MET TEST GRAMMAR, READING, AND WRITING PRACTICE TESTS WITH GRAMMAR & READING EXERCISES AND MICHIGAN ENGLISH TEST ESSAY SAMPLES

Michigan English Test and MET are trademarks of Michigan Language Assessment, in conjunction with Cambridge Assessment English, which are neither affiliated with nor endorse this publication and its related websites.

MET Test Grammar, Reading, and Writing Practice Tests with Grammar and Reading Exercises and Michigan English Test Essay Samples

© COPYRIGHT 2019 MET Test Success Associates dba www.michigan-test.com

All rights reserved. No part of this publication may be reproduced, stored in a retrieval system, or transmitted, in any form or by any means, electronic, mechanical, photocopying, recording, or otherwise, without the prior written permission of the copyright owner.

ISBN-13: 978-1-949282-31-3

ISBN-10: 1-949282-31-7

Michigan English Test and MET are trademarks of Michigan Language Assessment, in conjunction with Cambridge Assessment English, which are neither affiliated with nor endorse this publication and its related websites.

COPYRIGHT NOTICE TO EDUCATORS

Please respect copyright law. Under no circumstances may you make copies of these materials for distribution to or use by students. Should you wish to use the materials with students, you are required to purchase a copy of this publication for each of your students.

TABLE OF CONTENTS

PART 1 – MET GRAMMAR REVIEW AND PRACTICE EXERCISES

Adverbs of Place – Location	1
Exercises – Adverbs of Location	4
Adverbs of Degree	5
Exercises – Adverbs of Degree	7
Another / Other / Others	8
Exercises – Another / Other / Others – Exercises	9
Comparatives and Superlatives	10
Exercises – Comparatives and Superlatives	11
Connectives – Linking Words and Subordination	12
Exercises – Connectives	19
Emphatic Form (Do and Did)	22
Exercises – Emphatic Form (Do and Did)	23
Gerunds and Infinitives	24
Exercises – Gerunds and Infinitives	28
Modal Verbs	29
Exercises – Modal Verbs	31
Negative Adverbial Clauses	32
Exercises – Negative Adverbial Clauses	35
Past Perfect	36
Exercises – Past Perfect	37
Perfect Infinitive	38
Exercises – Perfect Infinitive	40
The Third Conditional	41
Exercises – Third Conditional	42
Pronouns in the Accusative Case	43
Exercise – Pronouns in the Accusative Case	44
Pronouns – Demonstrative and Relative Pronouns	45
Exercise – Demonstrative and Relative Pronouns	47
Phrasal Verbs and Prepositions	48
Phrasal Verbs – Exercise 1	49
Phrasal Verbs – Exercise 2	52
Phrasal Verbs – Exercise 3	53

Phrasal Verbs – Exercise 4	54
Prepositions – Exercises	55
Review of Verb Usage and Tense	57
Grammar Review Exercises – Set 1	65
Grammar Review Exercises – Set 2	68
Grammar Review Exercises – Set 3	71

PART 2 – MET READING TIPS AND EXERCISES

Strategies and Reading Tips for the MET Test	74
Reading Exercises:	
Main Idea	75
Specific Details	77
Implication or Inference	79
Vocabulary in Context	81
Author's Tone or Purpose	82

PART 3 – MET READING AND GRAMMAR PRACTICE TESTS

MET Reading and Grammar Practice Test 1	84
MET Reading and Grammar Practice Test 2	98

PART 4 – MET WRITING PRACTICE TESTS AND SAMPLE ESSAYS

Format of the MET Writing Test	112
Essay Scoring	113
Avoid Common Essay Errors and Raise Your Score	115
How to Organize and Structure Your MET Essay	117
MET Writing Test – Sample Response 1	118
Analysis of Essay Sample Response 1	120
MET Writing Test – Sample Response 2	122
Analysis of Essay Sample Response 2	124

10 MORE MET PRACTICE WRITING TESTS — 126

ANSWER KEYS

Grammar Exercises – Answers	130
Grammar Review Exercises – Answers	147
MET Reading and Grammar Practice Tests – Answers and Explanations	149

PART 1 – MET GRAMMAR REVIEW AND PRACTICE EXERCISES

Adverbs of Place – Location

You will probably see one or two questions on adverbs of location on the grammar section of the MET Test.

The function of adverbs of location is to state where things happen. They are sometimes also referred to as spatial adverbs.

Adverbs of location include the following:

- anyplace
- anyplace else
- anywhere
- anywhere else
- another place
- elsewhere
- everywhere
- somewhere
- somewhere else

When using an adverb of location with "I'd rather," be sure to use one with the word "else" or "another" since you are making a comparison.

ADVERBS OF LOCATION FOR COMPARISON

Elsewhere / somewhere else / another place

These three adverbs indicate that you may have other preferences in mind, besides the location already mentioned.

Example 1:

> The weather is going to be bad in New York this weekend, so I'd rather go elsewhere.

Example 2:

> The weather is going to be bad in New York this weekend, so I'd rather go somewhere else.

Example 3:

> The weather is going to be bad in New York this weekend, so I'd rather go another place.

Anywhere else / anyplace else

These two adverbs indicate that you don't have another preference in mind. Your mind is completely open to other ideas.

Example 4:

> The weather is going to be bad in New York this weekend, so I'd rather go anywhere else.

Example 5:

> The weather is going to be bad in New York this weekend, so I'd rather go anyplace else.

RMEMBER: When you use the word "else" you must be making a comparison in the sentence to another location.

ADVERBS OF LOCATION – NONCOMPARATIVE

Anyplace / anywhere / everywhere / somewhere

These adverbs are used when you are not making a comparison in the sentence.

Example 6:

> I'll go anyplace you want.

> I'll go anywhere you want.

Use "anyplace" when the speaker has no other preference.

Example 7:

> Your keys must be somewhere.

Use "somewhere" when you are not sure of the exact location.

Example 8:

> Pollen is everywhere this time of year.

Use "everywhere" when you want to show that the location is extremely common.

Now try the exercises on the next page.

Exercises – Adverbs of Location

Put one of the adverbs of location in the following sentences. Some sentences may have more than one correct answer. The answers to these exercises are provided at the back of the book.

anyplace / anyplace else / anywhere / anywhere else / another place / elsewhere / everywhere / somewhere / somewhere else

1) I don't know where I left my book. It could be _____.

2) Dallas is going to be so busy today. I'd rather go _____ , like Houston or Austin.

3) The doctor said the flu is very widespread this year because the virus is _____.

4) I just detest that restaurant. I'll go _____ !

5) I remember using that pair of scissors just a minute ago, so they must be _____ in the house.

6) He lost his keys when he was out, so they could be _____.

7) I don't like getting coffee in the mall, so I'd rather go _____ , like that cafe in town.

8) I dropped that pen while I was sitting at the desk, so it must be here _____ in the office.

9) I can't stand going to her house. I'd go _____ . I don't care where!

10) With these freezing temperatures, ice is _____ outside this time of year.

Adverbs of Degree

You will probably see at least one question on adverbs of degree on the grammar section of the MET Test.

The function of adverbs of degree is to state the intensity or degree of something.

Adverbs of degree are normally placed before the adjective or verb that they modify. However, there are some exceptions to this rule.

Here are some adverbs of degree and their rules of use.

TYPE 1: These adverbs must be placed before an adjective or adjectival phrase:

absolutely – to indicate the strongest or highest intensity of feeling

    I felt absolutely intimidated at that job interview.

    She was absolutely in love with him.

quite – to indicate a weaker intensity of feeling

    That movie was quite good, but I preferred the one we saw last week.

TYPE 2: The following adverbs must be placed before an adjective. They can also be used to modify a verb.

almost – to indicate that something is nearly complete

    The meal was almost ready.

    We have almost finished putting up wallpaper in our dining room.

barely – to indicate that something has only just been achieved.

    She was barely ten years old when her mother died.

    We could barely hear what the teacher was saying.

even – to intensify consequences or outcomes

    Your letter wasn't even professional because it had so many mistakes.

    Your lack of studying might even cause you to fail the exam.

hardly – to indicate the negative. Usage is similar to the word "not."

> Your lack of interest in me is hardly endearing.

> This small room can hardly be called a suite.

nearly – to indicate that something almost happened. Similar to "almost."

> The meal was nearly ready.

> We have nearly finished putting up wallpaper in our dining room.

EXCEPTIONS:

far – requires a comparative adjective

> It would be far better to talk about your problem with someone.

enough – must be used after an adjective or adverb

> He couldn't walk fast enough.

NOTES:

Be sure not to confuse adverbs of degree with adverbs of time, such as "just," "soon," "still," and "yet."

Adverbs of time indicate when something was done, rather than the intensity.

Now try the exercises on the next page.

Exercises – Adverbs of Degree

Put one of the adverbs of degree in the following sentences. Some sentences may have more than one correct answer. The answers to these exercises are provided at the back of the book.

absolutely / almost / barely / far / enough / even / hardly / nearly / quite

1) This jacket isn't big _____ for me.

2) You are _____ right about the situation.

3) In my opinion, pizza is _____ better than spaghetti.

4) He was _____ ready to go out; he only needed to put on his jacket.

5) He _____ fell off the edge of that cliff.

6) She was in serious condition at the hospital and _____ survived the accident.

7) We are _____ finished preparing the meal, so please sit at the table.

8) That old-fashioned dress can _____ be considered glamorous.

9) Your stupid remark wasn't _____ funny.

10) That outfit is _____ nice, but I prefer the other one.

Another / Other / Others

SINGLUAR ADJECTIVES

"Another" and "other" are adjectives and are singular.

Look at these examples:

    I would like another coffee, please.

"Another" is singular and modifies the noun "coffee."

    If the choice is between these two things, then I prefer the other one.

"Other" is an adjective and modifies "one" or "thing."

PLURAL PRONOUN

"Others" is a pronoun and is plural. "Other" can modify a plural noun.

Look at these examples:

    I like this painting, but there are many others in this museum.

"Others" is a plural pronoun which refers to the different paintings in the museum.

    Bill has three other sisters beside Berta.

"Other" is singular and modifies the noun "sisters."

USE AT END OF SENTENCE

"Another" and "other" can also be used at the end of a sentence, as shown in the following examples:

    He already has two dogs, but would still like another.

"Another" is singular, so in other words, he wants one more dog.

    Some people worry about health problems more than others.

"Others" is a plural pronoun that refers to other people.

Now try the exercises on the next page.

Exercises – Another / Other / Others

Complete the sentences with another, other, or others. The answers to these exercises are provided at the back of the book.

1) He has one house, but he wants to get _____ .

2) One student in the class wanted to go to a movie, but many _____ wanted to go bowling.

3) Some people like going to the beach more than _____ .

4) The family already has five adopted children, but would like _____ .

5) The choice so limited; I would prefer _____ options.

6) I had to decide between this jacket or the _____ one I have.

7) I like him, but _____ people don't like him so much.

8) I enjoy the rain, but _____ feel sad on rainy days.

9) James thought the book was great, but _____ friend of mine hated it.

10) Some people are more concerned than _____ about the potential tax increase.

Comparatives and Superlatives

The comparative form is used to compare two people or things. The things must be from the same group or category.

COMPARATIVES

EXAMPLE: Mary is the nicer of the two sisters.

In this example, Mary and her sister form one group.

The comparative form is also used to compare a person or thing to a group from which it is considered separate.

EXAMPLE: Mary is nicer than her three sisters.

There are four sisters. Mary is in one category. The three remaining sisters are in another category.

SUPERLATIVES

The superlative form is used to compare a person or thing to a group from which it is considered a member.

EXAMPLE: Mary is the nicest of her four sisters.

All four sisters are considered to be in the same category.

NOTES:

Remember to use the definite article ("the") with the superlative.

Double comparatives and double superlatives are grammatically incorrect.

INCORRECT: She is more prettier than her sister.

INCORRECT: She is the most prettiest in the family.

Now try the exercises on the next page.

Exercises – Comparatives and Superlatives

Complete the sentences with the comparative or superlative form of the given adjective. You may need to add "a," "the," "of," and "than" if necessary. The answers to these exercises are provided at the back of the book.

1) Professor Smith is _____ man I know.   INTELLIGENT

2) Professor Smith is _____ any other man I know. INTELLIGENT

3) Nancy is _____ her five sisters.   BEAUTIFUL

4) Nancy is _____ the six sisters.   BEAUTIFUL

5) Paul is _____ boy in his class.   SMART

6) Paul is _____ the other boys in his class.   SMART

7) They made Mary Jo manager because she worked _____ the other employees.   HARD

8) They made Mary Jo manager because she worked _____ all the employees.   HARD

9) Beth is _____ any other girl on the volleyball team.   TALL

10) Beth is _____ girl on the volleyball team.   TALL

Connectives – Linking Words and Subordination

Sentence linking words can help you combine short sentences together to create more complex sentence structures.

This skill is assessed on both the grammar and writing sections of the MET Test.

Sentence linking words and phrases fall into three categories:

- sentence linkers
- phrase linkers
- subordinators

In order to understand how to use these types of sentence linking words and phrases correctly, you will need to know some basics of English grammar.

Please study the examples below carefully before you do the exercises.

SENTENCE LINKERS

Sentence linkers are used to link two complete sentences together.

A complete sentence is one that has a grammatical subject and a verb.

Sentence linkers are usually placed at the beginning of a sentence and are followed by a comma.

They can also be preceded by a semicolon and followed by a comma when joining two sentences together. When doing so, the first letter of the first word of the second sentence must not be capitalized.

Now look at the following examples.

Sentence linker examples:

You need to enjoy your time at college. *However*, you should still study hard.

You need to enjoy your time at college; *however*, you should still study hard.

In the examples above, the grammatical subject of the first sentence is "you" and the verb is "need to enjoy."

In the second sentence, "you" is the grammatical subject and "should study" is the verb.

PHRASE LINKERS

In order to understand the difference between phrase linkers and sentence linkers, you must first be able to distinguish a sentence from a phrase.

A phrase linker must be followed by a phrase, while a sentence linker must be followed by a sentence.

Remember that a phrase does not have both a grammatical subject and a verb, while sentences contain grammatical subjects and verbs.

Here are some examples of phrases:

- her beauty and grace
- life's little problems
- a lovely summer day in the month of June
- working hard
- being desperate for money

Note that the last two phrases above use the –ing form, known in these instances as the present participle.

Present participle phrases, which are often used to modify nouns or pronouns, are sometimes placed at the beginning of sentences as introductory phrases.

Here are some examples of sentences:

Mary worked all day long.

My sister lives in Seattle.

Wintertime is brutal in Montana.

"Mary," "my sister," and "wintertime" are the grammatical subjects of the above sentences.

Remember that verbs are words that show action or states of being, so "worked," "lives," and "is" are the verbs in the three sentences above.

Look at the examples that follow:

> *Phrase linker example 1 – no comma:* He received a promotion *because of* his dedication to the job.

"His dedication to the job" is a noun phrase.

> *Phrase linker example 2 – with comma: Because of* his dedication to the job, he received a promotion.

When the sentence begins with the phrase linker, we classify the sentence as an inverted sentence.

Notice that you will need to place a comma between the two parts of the sentence when it is inverted.

SUBORDINATORS

Subordinators must be followed by an independent clause. Subordinators cannot be followed by a phrase.

The two clauses of a subordinated sentence must be separated by a comma.

The structure of independent clauses is similar to that of sentences because independent clauses contain a grammatical subject and a verb.

Subordinator examples:

> Although he worked hard, he failed to make his business profitable.
>
> He failed to make his business profitable, although he worked hard.

There are two clauses: "He worked hard" and "he failed to make his business profitable."

The grammatical subjects in each clause are the words "he", while the verbs are "worked" and "failed."

Now look at the linking words and phrases on the following pages. Note which ones are sentence linkers, which ones are phrase linkers, and which ones are subordinators. Then refer to the rules above to remember the grammatical principles for sentence linkers, phrase linkers, and subordinators.

Sentence linkers for additional information

further

furthermore

apart from this

what is more

in addition

additionally

in the same way

moreover

Sentence linkers for giving examples

for example

for instance

in this case

in particular

more precisely

namely

in brief

in short

Sentence linkers for stating the obvious

obviously

clearly

naturally

of course

surely

after all

simply

quite simply

Sentence linkers for giving conclusions

finally

to conclude

lastly

in conclusion

Sentence linkers for giving generalizations

in general

on the whole

as a rule

as often happens

as often as not

for the most part

generally speaking

in most cases

to the best of my knowledge

Sentence linkers for stating causes and effects

thus

accordingly

hence

therefore

in that case

under those circumstances

as a result

for this reason

as a consequence

consequently

in effect

Sentence linkers for concession or unexpected results

however

nevertheless

meanwhile

Sentence linkers for contrast

on the other hand

on the contrary

alternatively

rather

Sentence linkers for paraphrasing or restating

in other words

that is to say

that is

Sentence linkers for similarity

similarly

in the same way

likewise

Phrase linkers for giving additional information

besides

in addition to

Phrase linkers for stating causes and effects

because of

due to

owing to

Phrase linkers for contrast

in contrast to

instead of

rather than

without

Phrase linkers for concession or unexpected results

but for

despite

in spite of

Phrase linkers for comparison

compared to

like

Subordinators

although

as

as much as

because

but

due to the fact that

even though

however much

in so much as

not only . . . but also

once

since

so

so that

unless

until

when

whereas

while

Time words that are both phrase linkers and subordinators

after

before

<u>Special cases</u>

yet – "yet" can be used as both a subordinator and as a sentence linker.

in order to – "in order to" must be followed by the base form of the verb.

thereby – "thereby" must be followed by the present participle.

Now try the exercises on the next page.

Exercises – Connectives

Look at the sets of sentences in the exercises below. Make new sentences, using the phrase linkers, sentence linkers, and subordinators provided. In many cases, you will need to create one single sentence from the sentences provided. You may need to change or delete some of the words in the original sentences. Be careful with capitalization and punctuation in your answers. The answers to these exercises are provided at the back of the book.

1) The temperature was quite high yesterday. It really didn't feel that hot outside.

   a) In spite of . . .

   b) The temperature . . . nevertheless . . .

2) Our star athlete didn't receive a gold medal in the Olympics. He had trained for competition for several years in advance.

   a) Our star athlete . . . although . . .

   b) Despite . . .

3) There are acrimonious relationships within our extended family. Our immediate family decided to go away on vacation during the holiday season to avoid these conflicts.

   a) Because of . . .

   b) Because . . .

   c) Due to the fact that . . .

4) My best friend had been feeling extremely sick for several days. She refused to see the doctor.

a) My best friend . . . however. . .

b) My best friend . . . but . . .

5) He generally doesn't like drinking alcohol. He will do so on social occasions.

a) While . . .

b) He generally . . . yet . . .

6) The government's policies failed to stimulate spending and expand economic growth. The country slipped further into recession.

a) The government's policies . . . thus . . .

b) The government's policies . . . so . . .

7) Students may attend certain classes without fulfilling a prerequisite. Students are advised of the benefit of taking at least one non-required introductory course.

a) Even though . . .

b) Students may attend . . . apart from this . . .

8) There have been advances in technology and medical science. Infant mortality rates have declined substantially in recent years.

a) Owing to . . .

b) Since . . .

9) It was the most expensive restaurant in town. It had rude staff and provided the worst service.

a) It was the most . . . besides

b) In addition to . . .

10) *Now combine these three sentences.*

The judge did not punish the criminal justly. He decided to grant a lenient sentence. He did not send out a message to deter potential offenders in the future.

a) Instead of . . . and thereby . . .

b) Rather than . . . in order to . . .

Before you attempt your answer for question 10, look for the cause and effect relationships among the three sentences.

Emphatic Form (Do and Did)

We can use "do" or "did" with the base form of the verb to make a statement more emphatic.

Remember that the base form of the verb is the infinitive without "to."

Examples of the base form of the verb: see, eat, love, enjoy

The statement must always be in the affirmative.

DID – SPECIFIC ACTION OR EVENT IN THE PAST

We use the word "did" to emphasize a specific event or action that occurred in the past.

Examples:

>I know you think he couldn't have been at the party, but I *did see* him.

>I said I wouldn't touch the cake, but I *did eat* two pieces of it.

DO / DOES – GENERALIZATIONS OR SPECIFIC ACTION IN THE PRESENT

We use "do" or "does" for generalizations or to emphasize a specific event or action that occurs in the present.

Examples:

>In spite of having been told to be on time repeatedly, he still *does run* late on occasion.

>Even though I don't really like spinach, but I *do eat* it sometimes.

The emphatic forms of the verbs are *highlighted* in the above sentences.

Notice that the other part of the sentence contains information that contradicts the statement made in the emphatic part.

Now try the exercises on the next page.

Exercises – Emphatic Form (Do and Did)

Put the correct form of the verbs in the sentences provided below. One of the verbs must be in the emphatic form. The other verb may need to be in the negative form. The answers to these exercises are provided at the back of the book.

1) I thought he wouldn't want _____ (go) in the pool, but he _____ (swim).

2) Our boss has been told _____ (treat) his members of staff well, but he still _____ (insult) us from time to time.

3) You say you _____ (love) him anymore, but your actions show that you _____ (love) him.

4) You claim that you _____ (like) cake, but you _____ (eat) it sometimes.

5) In spite of _____ (leaving) very early, we _____ (arrive) late.

6) Even though she _____ (love) her children, she _____ (shout) at them terribly sometimes.

7) Although we _____ (repair) the car last week, it _____ (break down) again.

8) You claim _____ (be) indifferent to the situation, but you _____ (care) about it.

9) He pretends _____ (detest) tobacco use, but he _____ (smoke) almost every day.

10) She says that she _____ (have) any musical talent, but she _____ (sing) very well.

Gerunds and Infinitives

A gerund is a verbal noun which ends in "ing", while the infinitive consists of "to" and the base form of the verb.

Some verbs always take an infinitive (to + verb) and some always take a gerund (the –ing form). However, some will take either.

Look at the following examples and study the lists that follow.

INFINITIVE

    CORRECT: Sarah decided to go out.

    INCORRECT: Sarah decided going out.

Here are some more examples of the infinitive:

    He agreed to pay half the cost.

    She refused to wait.

    The man had chosen not to buy a ticket.

GERUND

    CORRECT: Sarah suggested going out.

    INCORRECT: Sarah suggested to go out.

Here are some more examples of the gerund:

    He recommended paying half the cost.

    I practice playing the piano.

    She admitted not buying a ticket.

Now study the infinitive and gerund list on the following pages.

These verbs and phrases take the infinitive:

advise	learn
agree	long
aim	manage
appear	mean
arrange	neglect
ask	offer
attempt	omit
be just about (ready)	pay
beg	plan
can't afford	prepare
can't wait	pretend
choose	promise
claim	prove
decide	refuse
demand	seem
enable	swear
expect	tend
fail	there's no reason
guarantee	threaten
happen	turn out
hesitate	want
hope	wish
it's time	

These verbs and phrases take the gerund:

admit	involve
appreciate	justify
avoid	keep
be in the habit of	keep on
be tired of	mention
can't help	miss
can't stand	not be worth
confess	postpone
consider	practice
contemplate	put off
delay	quit
deny	recommend
detest	resent
dislike	resist
don't mind	risk
enjoy	save
escape	suggest
excuse	thinking about
finish	thought of
give up	tolerate
have trouble	
How about . . .?	
imagine	

These verbs can take either the infinitive or the gerund: start, continue, intend, like and hate.

For example, both of these sentences as are correct:

    Andrew started to unpack his suitcase.

    Andrew started unpacking his suitcase.

Finally, remember that gerunds are used to speak about hobbies.

    I enjoy swimming.

    He can't stand hiking.

Now try the exercises on the next page.

Exercises – Gerunds and Infinitives

Complete the following sentences by using either the gerund or infinitive form of the verb provided. The answers to these exercises are provided at the back of the book.

1) It's not worth (write) the whole letter over again.

2) Gunther refused (listen) to what we had to say.

3) He denied (steal) the stereo.

4) Martina is in the habit of (stay up) quite late.

5) I advise you (study) more.

6) He was just about (leave) when the telephone rang.

7) I apologize. I meant (tell) you about the party last week.

8) How about (go) to a movie tonight?

9) I always have trouble (tie) this necktie.

10) As your manager, my job is checking (see) that you carry out your responsibilities.

11) The pianist is paid (play) music for the customers.

12) I have been thinking about (visit) my grandma next week.

13) She really enjoys (swim) in the summer.

14) It's time (pack) our things and head home.

15) There's no reason (cry) about it.

16) I'm really tired of (hear) him complain all the time.

17) Have you ever considered (cut) your hair short?

18) I hope (win) the lottery and live in Brazil someday.

19) Imagine (have) a million dollars!

20) You must be prepared (study) a lot if you want to succeed at college.

Modal Verbs

You may see questions on the grammar part of the test on modal verbs. Modal verbs are used to express obligation, certainty, possibility, or permission. Most commonly, the test assesses the modal verbs "should," "would," "might," and "could." However, sometimes other modal verbs such as "can," "may," or "must" are also included on the exam.

can

The modal verb "can" is used to show permission or possibility.

    A general possibility: Learning a language can be difficult.

    Permission: I can drive her car when she is out of town.

The word "can" is also used in passive sentence constructions, like in the examples below.

    Example – Active voice: You can declare that income on your tax return.

    Example – Passive voice: That income can be declared on your tax return.

could

The modal verb "could" is used to make suggestions and polite requests, as well as to talk about past possibilities and future possibilities.

    Suggestion: You could spend your holiday in Thailand.

    Polite request: Could I read that book when you have finished it?

    Past possibility: I could have failed the examination. I certainly hadn't studied enough for it.

    Future possibility: He could be found guilty of the crime when the police have finished their investigation.

may

The modal verb "may" is used to talk about present or future possibilities or to give permission.

    Present possibility: She may be upset right now, so I wouldn't tell her more bad news.

    Future possibility: She may be upset if you decide to lie to her.

    Permission: You may leave the table when you have finished eating.

might

The modal verb "might" is used to talk about future possibilities. It can also be used to talk about past possibilities.

Future possibility: She might take a taxi home since the party is going to finish late.

Past possibility: I might have failed the driving test. I certainly didn't feel prepared.

must

The modal verb "must" is used to express certainty or necessity.

Certainty: That must have been the restaurant. It's the only one on the street.

Necessity (for something that is necessary): You must have a valid library card to check out a book.

should

The word "should" is used to give advice or to express expectation or obligation. "Should" needs to be used with another verb.

Advice: You should study hard for your exam.

Expectation: You should be able to finish the work within three days.

Obligation: You should have returned the video on time. Now you will have to pay a late fee.

would

The modal verb "would" can be used to express one's thoughts on an action in the past. Be sure to avoid the "would of" construction, which is not grammatical.

CORRECT: I would have studied more if I had known the exam was going to be so difficult.

INCORRECT: I would of studied more if I had known the exam was going to be so difficult.

The correct sentence above containing "would" is an example of the third conditional sentence structure.

Now try the exercises on the next page.

Exercises – Modal Verbs

Complete the following sentences, placing modal verbs in the space provided. Some sentences may have more than one answer. The answers to these exercises are provided at the back of the book.

1) You _____ have told us you weren't coming. We waited for over an hour. OBLIGATION

2) There are several ways to get to Boston from here. You _____ even take the train. SUGGESTION

3) Paloma said she _____ / _____ / _____ be going to the picnic tomorrow. She wasn't sure. FUTURE POSSIBILITY

4) You have a terrible cough. You _____ go to the doctor. ADVICE

5) He _____ have gone out for the night. He's not answering the phone. CERTAINTY

6) _____ / _____ / _____ I have another slice of cake, please? PERMISSION (2) / POLITE REQUEST (1)

7) The weather forecast said it _____ / _____ / _____ rain tomorrow. FUTURE POSSIBILITY

8) A good mother _____ / _____ always be concerned with the welfare of her children. NECESSITY (1) / ADVICE (1)

9) All residents _____ pay taxes if they have an income – it's the law. NECESSITY

10) What an awful accident. We _____ / _____ have been killed. PAST POSSIBILITY

Negative Adverbial Clauses

When a sentence begins with a negative adverb, the auxiliary verb is inverted. In other words, the auxiliary verb is placed in front of the grammatical subject of the sentence, instead of being in its usual position, which is next to the main verb. Therefore, an inverted sentence follows this pattern:

Negative adverb + auxiliary verb + grammatical subject + main verb

Look at this example and notice how it follows the pattern given above:

Not only do sports exist as a source of entertainment for the public, but also as a lucrative business enterprise for those who provide financial backing.

Not only (negative adverb) + do (auxiliary verb) + sports (grammatical subject) + exist (main verb)

If the adverbial this sentence were not inverted, it would look like this:

Sports exist not only as a source of entertainment for the public, but also as a lucrative business enterprise for those who provide financial backing.

Notice that the word "do" is added when the sentence is inverted.

Here are some negative adverbs that are commonly encountered on the MET examination:

- never
- never before
- not
- only when
- only once
- seldom
- rarely
- hardly ever

These negative adverbs can be placed into five categories.

TYPE 1: If the original sentence contains an auxiliary verb, such as "would," "had," or "did" the auxiliary verb is inverted.

Example:

    Original sentence: I had seen her only once before then.

    Inverted sentence: Only once before then had I seen her.

TYPE 2: If the original sentence does not contain an auxiliary verb, the verb "do" is used in the inverted sentence.

Example:

    Original sentence: Sarah not only failed the driving test, she also had an accident.

    Inverted sentence: Not only did Sarah fail the driving test, she also had an accident.

TYPE 3: If the original sentence is in the negative (i.e., if it contains the words "not" or "never"), the negative word is placed at the beginning of the inverted sentence.

Examples:

    Original sentence: Mary didn't tell a single person her secret.

    Inverted sentence: Not a single person did Mary tell her secret.

    Original sentence: I have never experienced anything like that before.

    Inverted sentence: Never before have I experienced anything like that.

TYPE 4: If the original sentence contains the word "when," the inverted sentence begins "Only when." You may also need to add "do" to the second part of the inverted sentence.

Example:

    Original sentence: John remembered his co-worker's name when they had finished their conversation.

Inverted sentence: Only when they had finished their conversation did John remember his co-worker's name.

TYPE 5: If the original sentence contains an adverb of frequency such as "often" or "not often," the inverted sentence can begin with "Seldom," "Rarely," or "Hardly ever."

Example:

Original sentence: Mark doesn't go on vacation often.

Inverted sentence: Rarely does Mark go on vacation.

Now try the exercises on the next page.

Exercises – Negative Adverbial Clauses

Write a new sentence as similar as possible in meaning to the sentence provided, using the negative adverbial phrases indicated below. It may be helpful to identify the type of sentence by looking at the previous examples. The answers to these exercises are provided at the back of the book.

1) Bread would not be available at the grocery store until noon.

    Not until . . .

2) Frank realized he had forgotten to fill up his truck when it ran out of gas.

    Only when . . .

3) I have never changed a flat tire in my life.

    Never before . . .

4) I realized who he was when he took off his sunglasses.

    Only when . . .

5) I have never seen such an exciting football game in my life.

    Never . . .

6) John didn't say a word during the entire drive home.

    Not . . .

7) A teenager seldom flunks his driving test the first time.

    Rarely . . .

8) Jane doesn't stay out past midnight very often.

    Seldom . . .

9) I have seen the Grand Canyon only one time.

    Only once . . .

10) He rarely has time to see his parents since he has gone away to college.

    Hardly ever . . .

Past Perfect

The past perfect is often used to express an action which has just recently occurred. It can also be used to show that one action preceded another when a sentence describes two actions.

When describing two actions, the past perfect is used for the action which happened first. The simple past is used for the subsequent action.

The past perfect is often used with the words "just" and "after," and with the phrase "no sooner . . . than."

Remember that the auxiliary verb must come before the word "just."

Example 1: When we had just arrived, she decided to leave.

Example 2: No sooner had we arrived than she decided to leave.

In both of the examples above, the arrival happened first. Immediately after that, she decided to leave.

"No sooner" is a negative adverbial. Accordingly, the auxiliary verb needs to be inverted in the second example sentence above.

So, in the second example sentence, we have to use the inverted structure "had we," instead of the normal structure "we had."

Now try the exercises on the next page

Exercises – Past Perfect

Change the verbs given in the following sentences, using the past perfect and the simple past tense. The answers to these exercises are provided at the back of the book.

1) No sooner _____ (we get) on the interstate highway than our car _____ (break down).

2) No sooner _____ (I finish) speaking on the phone than the doorbell _____ (ring).

3) Someone _____ (tell) Bethany before I _____ (have) a chance to tell her myself.

4) Carlos _____ (tear up) that note after I _____ (see) it.

5) I _____ (see) the wedding dress you _____ (choose).

6) She _____ (receive) the letter several days after I _____ (mail) it.

7) No sooner _____ (the fire start) than the alarm _____ (go off).

8) After Lamar _____ (become) sleepy, he _____ (leave) the party.

9) Just when the party _____ (begin), we _____ (see) Nancy come in the door.

10) I _____ (just say) goodbye to Suki when Bao Yu _____ (arrive).

Perfect Infinitive

The perfect infinitive is often assessed on the grammar part of the MET Test.

It is formed as follows: verb + to + has / have + past participle

Usage with Common Verbs

The perfect infinitive is often used after the following words:

claim, expect, hate, hope, like, love, want, pretend

Look at these examples:

> She claimed to have lost her phone when we were out last week.
>
> He pretended to have decided what to do, although I knew he hadn't.

Past Usage

As in the examples above, the perfect infinitive often refers to events that have taken place in the past.

Look at more examples:

> I feel privileged to have worked here for the past five years.
>
> He was lucky enough to have lived in Paris.

Future Usage

The perfect infinitive can also refer to things that will take place in the future.

Look at these examples:

> We hope to have finished the job by the end of the month
>
> She wants to have lost five pounds before she goes on vacation.

Passive Form

The perfect infinitive also has a passive form.

The perfect infinitive passive is formed as follows:

> verb + to + has / have + + been + past participle

The passive form of the perfect infinitive is often used after the following words:

believe, said, claim, like, love, understand

Look at this example:

These caves are said to have been formed over millions of years.

Now try the exercises on the next page.

Exercises – Perfect Infinitive

Complete the sentences with the perfect infinitive form of the given verb. You may need to use either the active or the passive form. The answers to these exercises are provided at the back of the book.

1) I wanted _____ (wear) something better to the surprise party last night, but I had nothing else packed in my suitcase.

2) She claimed _____ (pass) her test, although he didn't believe her.

3) I pretended _____ (enjoy) myself after going to that party, but I really detested it.

4) I feel so lucky _____ (visit) London on vacation last year.

5) Some of our oldest laws are said _____ (influence) by those from ancient Greece.

6) He passed away recently, but I was happy _____ (know) him so well during his lifetime.

7) We hope _____ (win) the championship when we on our way home from the tournament next week.

8) I feel fortunate _____ (love) by a wonderful spouse for forty years.

9) She hopes _____ (be) on her vacation for four days by this time next week.

10) The geological features are said _____ (change) over time by the flow of water in the area.

The Third Conditional

The third conditional is used to hypothesize, or make a guess about, how a past event could have happened differently. The following structure is used:

If + past perfect . . . would + have + past participle

The past perfect structure is sometimes inverted on the MET examination.

Inversion involves removing the word "if" from the original sentence and beginning the new sentence with the word "had."

Look at this example:

Had she not been so careless, the fire would not have started.

This sentence has been inverted. It could be re-written as follows:

If she had not been so careless, the fire would not have started.

The word "might" can be used instead of "would":

Had she not been so careless, the fire might not have started.

If she had not been so careless, the fire might not have started.

"Might" indicates that the outcome was possible. "Would" indicates that the outcome was definite.

Now try the exercises on the next page.

Exercises – Third Conditional

Write one sentence for each of the following groups of sentences, using the inverted third conditional structure. You may need to add or remove the word "not" from either clause of the sentence you make. The answers to these exercises are provided at the back of the book.

1) Marek didn't drive carefully. He had an accident.

   Had Marek . . .

2) Pavel decided not to buy the car. She didn't like it.

   Had Pavel . . .

3) I didn't pass my exam. I didn't study for it.

   Had I . . .

4) Dasha didn't wear a sweater. She caught a cold.

   Had Dasha . . .

5) I didn't prepare anything to eat. I didn't know you were coming.

   Had I . . .

6) Zahra was so bored by the TV program. She fell asleep.

   Had Zahra . . .

7) The movie wasn't interesting. I left half-way through.

   Had the movie . . .

8) I told my friend he was stupid. He left in a rage.

   Had I not . . .

9) He argued with his boss. As a result, he was fired.

   Had he not . . .

10) It rained all night. The football game was canceled.

    Had it not . . .

Pronouns in the Accusative Case

The pronoun "I" is in the nominative case and should be used as a grammatical subject. You should use "I" last if you are naming more than one person in the grammatical subject.

Example: Sung Li, Marta, and I went shopping last Wednesday.

The word "me" is in the accusative case and should be used as an object.

Example: Tom emailed me yesterday.

MORE THAN ONE GRAMMATICAL OBJECT

Confusion sometimes occurs when more than one person is mentioned as the object of the sentence.

CORRECT: I told you to send Tom and me a copy of the letter.

INCORRECT: I told you to send Tom and I a copy of the letter.

AFTER PREPOSITIONS

Also be sure to use the accusative case after prepositions.

CORRECT: Between you and me, I'm not sure whether to believe her story.

INCORRECT: Between you and I, I'm not sure whether to believe her story.

OTHER PRONOUNS

The same rules apply to he / him, she / her, they / them, and we / us.

Example: Sung Li, Marta, and she went shopping last Wednesday.

I told you to send a copy of the letter to Tom and him.

I told you to send a copy of the letter to them and us

Now try the exercises on the next page.

Exercise – Pronouns in the Accusative Case

Put the correct form of the pronoun in the gaps in the sentences below. The answers to these exercises are provided at the back of the book.

1) He doesn't want to get involved because this problem is between you and _____ (first person).

2) That issue needs to be discussed at a meeting with all of you and _____ (second person masculine).

3) The tour of the factory for you and _____ (first person) will take place at 9:00 AM tomorrow.

4) If you had wanted to speak to her, you should have said something when you and _____ (third person feminine) were together yesterday.

5) Because we weren't invited to his party, he didn't get a birthday present from either _____ (third person feminine) or _____ (first person).

6) I don't want to argue with you or _____. (third person masculine)

7) He wants to give the instructions to her, you, and _____ (first person) all together in order to save time.

8) In case you need something else from us, just call either _____ (third person feminine) or _____ . (first person)

9) I simply couldn't believe her after all of the lies she has told you and _____ (first person).

10) She seems to hold something against us because you and _____ (first person) got better grades than she did.

Pronouns – Demonstrative and Relative Pronouns

DEMONSTRATIVE PRONOUNS

Demonstrative pronouns include the following words: this, that, these, those

This / That

"This" is used for a singular item that is nearby. "That" is used for singular items that are further away in time or space.

    Singular: This book that I have here is really interesting.

    Plural: That book on the table over there is really interesting.

These / Those

"These" is used for plural items that are nearby. "Those" is used for plural items that are further away in time or space.

    Singular: These pictures on my phone were taken on our vacation.

    Plural: Those pictures on the wall were taken on our vacation.

Avoid using "them" instead of "those":

INCORRECT: Them pictures on the wall were taken on our vacation.

RELATIVE PRONOUNS

Relative pronouns include the following: which, that, who, whom, whose

"Which" and "that" are used to describe things, and "who" and "whom" are used to describe people. "Whose" is used for people or things.

Which / That / Who

    WHICH: Last night, I watched a romantic-comedy movie which was really funny.

    THAT: Last night, I watched a romantic-comedy movie that was really funny.

    WHO: Susan always remains calm under pressure, unlike Tom, who is always so nervous.

"Who" is used because we are describing the person. This is known as the nominative case.

Whom / Whose

WHOM: To whom should the report be given?

"Whom" is used because the person is receiving an action, which is receiving the report. This is known as the accusative case.

WHOSE: I went out for lunch with Marta, whose parents are from Costa Rica.

WHOSE: I went out for lunch yesterday at that new restaurant, whose name I don't remember.

Now try the exercises on the next page.

Exercise – Demonstrative and Relative Pronouns

Complete the sentences with the following words: this, that, these, those, that, which, who, whom, whose. Some sentences may have more than one answer. The answers to these exercises are provided at the back of the book.

1) Last night, I read a graphic novel _____ was really interesting.

2) She has only one sister, _____ lives in Los Angeles.

3) _____ magazine, _____ I have here in my hand, is so boring.

4) _____ day last week was one of the worst days of my life.

5) His brother, _____ name is Samuel, is studying to become a lawyer.

6) I need to wear _____ gloves in the closet upstairs when I go out.

7) If you would like to know what my daughter looks like, have a look at _____ pictures right here.

8) I wanted to deliver the project, but I wasn't informed to _____ it should be given.

9) That city, _____ name I can't remember, is on the border of Kansas and Missouri.

10) She told everyone my secret, _____ really annoyed me.

Phrasal Verbs and Prepositions

Many students struggle with phrasal verbs and prepositions.

Indeed, even advanced-level learners of English can have difficulties with these skills.

Unlike verb tense and form, phrasal verbs and prepositions generally cannot be classified into categories of usage according to situations or time.

In other words, phrasal verb and preposition usage cannot really be explained.

They are something that simply needs to be learned from memory.

So, for phrasal verbs, you will need to learn each verb and its particle, as well as its meaning, by studying and memorizing them.

Likewise, you will need to remember that certain nouns, verbs, and adjectives are used with only one particular preposition.

The exercises on the following pages will help refresh your skills with phrasal verbs and prepositions.

Phrasal Verbs – Exercise 1

Place the missing particle or particles in the phrasal verbs given in the following sentences. A definition is given to help you. The answers to these exercises are provided at the back of the book.

1) I ran _____ Debbie at the mall yesterday. (ENCOUNTERED)

2) I'm not dating him anymore. We broke_____ two weeks ago. (FINISH A RELATIONSHIP)

3) What's the point of trying? I give_____ . (SURRENDER)

4) Mary Beth has taken _____ the management of the corporation. (TAKEN CONTROL OF)

5) I'm kind of old-fashioned. You see, I was brought _____ on a farm. (RAISED)

6) Our pick-up truck broke _____ in the middle of Route 66. (CEASED TO FUNCTION)

7) We looked down at the terminal as the airplane took _____ . (ASCENDED)

8) The coach tried to bring her _____ after she fainted during the basketball game. (HELP TO REGAIN CONSCIOUSNESS)

9) I don't see how he got _____ _____ cheating on the final last semester. (REMAINED FREE FROM BLAME)

10) The majority of the runners could not keep _____ _____ the leader in the marathon. (MAINTAIN THE PACE)

11) Car alarms that give_____ those squealing noises annoy me. (EMIT)

12) The salary and benefits package your company has offered is quite generous. I would, however, like a few days to think the matter _____ . (CONTEMPLATE)

13) After further consideration, I have decided to turn _____ your offer. (REJECT)

14) Where is Jim? Perhaps he got held _____ in a traffic jam somewhere. (DELAYED)

15) First, his company went bankrupt, and now all his friends have turned _____ him. (BETRAYED)

16) He must be the most benevolent man on earth. He is always giving money _____ to charity. (CONTRIBUTING)

17) I'd advise you to steer clear of her. You'll only have trouble if you get mixed _____ in her problems. (GET INVOLVED)

18) The baseball game was put _____ until Friday due to the bad weather. (POSTPONED)

19) It's taken you forever to get _____ your cold. (RECOVER)

20) I wasn't ready to get up when my alarm went _____ this morning. (SOUNDED)

21) Have you heard the news? An epidemic has broken _____. (OCCURRED)

22) If the snow would hold _____ for a few days, they could clear a pass through the mountains. (CEASE TEMPORARILY)

23) The government should do something about the current rate of inflation. Prices are constantly going _____ . (INCREASING)

24) You need to cut _____ _____ your intake of saturated fat or you'll have a heart attack. (REDUCE)

25) He told me to look him _____ if I'm ever in Dallas on business. (LOCATE)

26) Their plans for a two-week vacation in Europe fell _____ at the last minute. (FAILED TO MATERIALIZE)

27) You're an imbecile if you believe that story. She's made the whole thing _____. (INVENTED, CREATED)

28) He constantly belittles her. He always makes her feel inferior by putting her _____ . (CRITICIZING)

29) I can't stay at your place all week. I don't want to put you _____ . (IMPOSE)

30) You're free to go now. We won't take _____ any more of your time. (USE, WASTE)

Phrasal Verbs – Exercise 2

Match the phrasal verb on the left to the correct meaning provided on the right. The answers to these exercises are provided at the back of the book.

1.	She just **barged into** the room without knocking.	A.	to make more talkative
2.	We all **chipped in** to buy Aisha a birthday present.	B.	to convert
3.	He is really very shy, but if you talk to him, you can **draw** him **out**.	C.	to enter without knocking
4.	They are going to **knock down** the old cinema next week.	D.	to cause
5.	They are **turning** their garage **into** an extra bedroom.	E.	to admire
6.	Do you know where I can **get a hold of** yesterday's newspaper?	F.	to acquire
7.	The college's fee increase nearly **brought about** a protest.	G.	to contribute
8.	Running that marathon really **did** me **in**.	H.	to cause exhaustion
9.	I really **look up to** you for your courage.	I.	to make a mistake
10.	I can ignore your error this time, but don't **slip up** again.	J.	to demolish

Phrasal Verbs – Exercise 3

1.	Raquel is far from taciturn. In fact, she can really **ramble on**.	A.	to require or necessitate
2.	None of the students knew what the professor was **driving at**.	B.	to locate with difficulty
3.	Being successful in business **calls for** insight and hard work.	C.	to create poor health
4.	You **bring on** most of your problems by yourself.	D.	to cease or stop
5.	Newspaper reporters are always trying to **dig up** gossip.	E.	to cause
6.	That really annoys me. I wish you would **cut it out**.	F.	to disapprove of something
7.	If you don't stop working so hard you will **run** yourself **down**.	G.	to revoke
8.	Smoking outside the hospital entrance is **frowned on**.	H.	to talk incessantly
9.	I thought that I wasn't going to like the party, but it **turned out** to be fun.	I.	to transpire or prove to be
10.	I hope you won't **go back on** your promise to help me.	J.	to mean something

Phrasal Verbs – Exercise 4

1.	Enrique **bailed out of** the agreement after having second thoughts.	A.	to withdraw from
2.	The football match was **called off** due to the rain.	B.	to locate something
3.	Why do you **keep on** doing that? I've told you a million times to stop.	C.	to choose
4.	Julia didn't **let on** that she knew about the surprise party.	D.	to audition for or test
5.	I had to wait at the town hall while they **brought up** my information on the computer.	E.	to reveal something
6.	Dave is such a bully. He shouldn't **pick on** people and be so mean.	F.	to provide transport in vehicle
7.	You can **pick out** any of the tomatoes you like.	G.	to persist
8.	Be ready at 8:00 sharp. I'll **pick** you **up** at the front door.	H.	to tease or torment
9.	Sarah is going to **try out** for the choir next week.	I.	to accept
10.	You shouldn't **take on** too many responsibilities.	J.	to cancel

Prepositions – Exercises

Place appropriate prepositions in the spaces provided. The answers to these exercises are provided at the back of the book.

1) After 25 years _____ marriage, she is still faithful _____ her husband and devoted _____ her children.

2) It took him several months to recover _____ his viral infection.

3) The politician was completely devoid _____ integrity.

4) The subject of building a new hotel is currently _____ discussion.

5) I was given office supplies, consisting _____ paper and pens.

6) She was really pleased _____ receiving first prize.

7) The success of any business is contingent _____ the strength of its management.

8) John hadn't expected such an icy reception. In fact, he was really taken _____ surprise.

9) You will never be healthy if your diet is deficient _____ vitamins.

10) Police officers are _____ duty all day long.

11) Could you give me a little help _____ my chemistry assignment?

12) She had gained so much weight that she was really ashamed _____ herself.

13) The manager will investigate the matter and will contact you _____ writing.

14) It was love at first sight. She fell _____ him the moment they first met.

15) That author is famous _____ his horror stories.

16) It has taken me a long time to get accustomed _____ living in this area.

17) She really loves her car and would hate to part _____ it.

18) Many species are threatened _____ extinction nowadays.

19) If you refuse to work hard, your endeavors will amount _____ nothing.

20) I hope you're going to stand _____ your promise.

21) Jamila is really pleased _____ Amir for being so cooperative.

22) Ali really likes listening _____ music in his free time.

23) Many homes are not insured _____ earthquake damage.

24) Will you exchange your old car _____ a different model?

25) His version of the story was not consistent _____ the facts.

26) You will be given a refund in accordance _____ the terms _____ the product warranty.

27) Six out _____ ten residents of this city have attended university.

28) I don't approve _____ your behavior.

29) I haven't been introduced _____ him, although I know him _____ sight.

30) Robert's company has always operated _____ a profit.

REVIEW OF VERB USAGE AND TENSE

ACTIVE VOICE

Present simple tense

The present simple tense is used for habitual actions.

> Example: He goes to the office at 8:00 every morning.

The present tense is also used to state facts or generalizations.

> Example: Water freezes at zero degrees Celsius.

The present simple tense is formed as follows:

- I work.
- You work.
- He / She / It works.
- We work.
- You work. (Plural)
- They work.

Past simple tense

The past simple tense is used for actions that were started and completed in the past.

> Example: I walked three miles yesterday.

The past simple tense is formed as follows:

- I worked.
- You worked.
- He / She / It worked.
- We worked.
- You worked. (Plural)
- They worked.

Please note that the previous example contains the regular verb "work." You should also be acquainted with the irregular verb forms for the exam.

Future simple tense

The future simple tense is used for actions that will occur in the future.

> Example: Jane will study in the evening tomorrow.

The future simple tense is formed as follows:

- I will work.
- You will work.
- He / She / It will work.
- We will work.
- You will work. (Plural)
- They will work.

Simple tenses:
Present simple – habits, truths, or generalizations
Past simple – actions completed in the past
Future simple – actions to be completed in the future

Present perfect tense

The present perfect tense is used for actions that were completed in the past, but that have relevancy in the present time.

> Example: I have studied every day this week.

The phrase "this week" shows that the action has relevancy in the present time.

The present perfect tense is formed as follows:

- I have worked.
- You have worked.
- He / She / It has worked.
- We have worked.

- You have worked. (Plural)
- They have worked.

Past perfect tense

The past perfect is often used for an action which has just recently occurred.

The past perfect form can also be used to show that one action preceded another when a sentence describes two past actions. In this situation, the past perfect is used for the action which happened first. The simple past is used for the subsequent action.

The past perfect is often used with the words "just" and "after" and with the phrase "no sooner . . . than."

   Example: I had just finished writing her an email when she called me.

There are two actions in the above sentence, but the action of writing was finished before the action of calling.

Remember that the auxiliary verb must come before the word "just."

   Example: We had just arrived, when she decided to leave.

"No sooner" is a negative adverbial. Accordingly, the auxiliary verb needs to be inverted in sentences that have this adverbial phrase.

   Example: No sooner had we arrived, than she decided to leave.

The past perfect tense is formed as follows:

- I had worked.
- You had worked.
- He / She / It had worked.
- We had worked.
- You had worked. (Plural)
- They had worked.

Future perfect tense

The future perfect tense is used to describe an action that will be completed at a definite time in the future.

Example: By this time next week, I will have finished all of my exams.

The future perfect tense is formed as follows:

- I will have worked.
- You will have worked.
- He / She / It will have worked.
- We will have worked.
- You will have worked. (Plural)
- They will have worked.

> **Perfect tenses:**
> Present perfect – actions completed in the past, but relevant in the present time
> Past perfect – an action in the past that is relevant in the present and was completed before another action in the past
> Future perfect – actions to be completed by a specific time in the future

Present simple progressive

The present simple progressive is used to describe actions that are in progress at the time of speaking.

Example: He is studying for his final exams right now.

The present simple progressive is also used to describe actions that will take place at a fixed time in the future.

Example: He is leaving for London on Tuesday.

The present simple progressive is formed as follows:

- I am working.
- You are working.
- He / She / It is working.

- We are working.
- You are working. (Plural)
- They are working.

Past simple progressive

The past simple progressive is used for actions that were in progress in the past.

The past simple progressive can be used to indicate that an action was in progress in the past when it was interrupted by a subsequent action.

    Example: I was cleaning the house yesterday when the doorbell rang.

The past simple progressive is formed as follows:

- I was working.
- You were working.
- He / She / It was working.
- We were working.
- You were working. (Plural)
- They were working.

Future simple progressive

The future simple progressive is used for actions that will be in progress in the future.

    Example: Jane will be traveling around the world next year.

The future simple tense is formed as follows:

- I will be working.
- You will be working.
- He / She / It will be working.
- We will be working.
- You will be working. (Plural)
- They will be working.

Present perfect progressive

The present perfect progressive is used for actions that were in progress in the past, but that have relevancy in the present time.

　　　　Example: I have been working very hard lately.

The phrase "lately" shows that the action has relevancy in the present time.

The present perfect progressive is formed as follows:

- I have been working.
- You have been working.
- He / She / It has been working.
- We have been working.
- You have been working. (Plural)
- They have been working.

> **Progressive forms:**
> Present simple progressive – action is in progress at the time of speaking or is to take place at a definite time in the future
> Past simple progressive – actions in progress in the past
> Future simple progressive – actions to be in progress in the future

PASSIVE VOICE

Use the passive voice to emphasize the object of the action, rather than the person doing the action or the action itself.

In the example sentences that follow in this section, the diplomas are the object of the action.

We want to emphasize the fact that the diplomas are being issued. We want to de-emphasize the fact that the university officials are the people responsible for handing out the diplomas.

In other words, we could write our example sentence in the active voice, like this:

Example (Active voice): The university officials hand out diplomas on graduation day every year.

Present simple passive

The present simple passive describes generalizations or things that normally occur in a predictable way.

Example: Diplomas are handed out on graduation day every year.

Past simple passive

The past simple passive is used to show that an action was completed in the past.

Example: Diplomas were handed out on graduation day last year.

Future simple passive

The future simple passive is used for events that will be completed in the future.

Example: Diplomas will be handed out on graduation day in May this year.

Future passive with is / are

The "future passive with is / are" is used in the sentence below because it describes an action that is planned for the future.

Example: Diplomas are to be handed out on graduation day in May this year.

Present simple progressive passive

The present simple progressive passive is used in the sentence below because we are talking about an action that will take place during a definite time in the future. This form emphasizes that a plan is in place for the event.

Example: Diplomas are being handed out on graduation day, which is May 18th this year.

Past simple progressive passive

The past simple progressive passive is used to show that an action was in progress in the past, and we want to put an emphasis on that action.

> Example: The diplomas were being handed out on graduation day when the ceremony was interrupted.

Present perfect passive

The present perfect passive is used in the sentence below because it emphasizes that the diplomas have been handed out like this in the past, and this action continues in the present.

> Example: Diplomas have been handed out on graduation day since the university was founded in 1924.

Past perfect passive

The past perfect passive is used in the following sentence because it emphasizes that the diplomas were handed out like this in the past, but the policy on handing out diplomas in this way has recently changed.

> Example: Diplomas had been handed out on graduation day until last year, when they started to be sent in the mail.

Now try the three sets of grammar review exercises on the following pages.

GRAMMAR REVIEW EXERCISES – SET 1

1. I don't know _____ the promotion or not.
    A. whether got
    B. he got
    C. if he got
    D. that he got

2. Bob is upset because he saw a bad accident that _____ this morning.
    A. was happening
    B. happened
    C. has happening
    D. happen

3. Someone once advised me _____ to California in the summer.
    A. not to go
    B. not going
    C. not go
    D. if I not go

4. _____ in reading popular novels.
    A. I am interesting
    B. Interesting it is
    C. I am interested
    D. It is interesting

5. That device is a machine _____ documents.
    A. by which transmits
    B. which are transmitted
    C. by which are transmitted
    D. which transmits

6. _____ her only once since she went away to college.
    A. I have seen
    B. Did I seen
    C. Have I seen
    D. I see

7. The last few months _____ their toll on him.
   A. taken
   B. have taken
   C. made
   D. have made

8. You would have passed your test _____ more.
   A. had you studied
   B. if you studied
   C. you had studied
   D. would you studied

9. That restaurant has dishes that aren't _____ anywhere else.
   A. to be served
   B. serving
   C. served
   D. to serve

10. _____ it, I can't really say if I like skiing.
    A. Never having tried
    B. Never had trying
    C. Never to have tried
    D. Never to try

11. She would have _____ in the accident had she not put on her seat belt.
    A. injury
    B. been injuring
    C. been injured
    D. to be injured

12. To _____ a long story short, I decided not to go to Los Angeles.
    A. take
    B. make
    C. taking
    D. making

13. People _____ about that new video.
    A. constant talk
    B. constant talking
    C. constantly to be talking
    D. are constantly talking

14. He was evicted from his apartment, but what _____ was pay his rent on time.
    A. he should do
    B. should he do
    C. he should have done
    D. he should be doing

15. The professor was telling us not _____ so much time talking.
    A. spending
    B. to be spending
    C. to spending
    D. be spending

GRAMMAR REVIEW EXERCISES – SET 2

1. We don't have any plans for tonight. How about _____ bowling?
   A. to go
   B. we go
   C. going for
   D. going

2. Teachers get tired of students _____ about how much homework they are given.
   A. to complain
   B. complaints
   C. to have complained
   D. complaining

3. If you want to go for a hamburger, I _____ one too.
   A. like to have
   B. feel like to have
   C. feel like having
   D. feel like I have had

4. The new fitness center _____ next week.
   A. be opening
   B. is being opening
   C. will opening
   D. is having its opening

5. Janet told me about the surprise party, although she _____ .
   A. mightn't have
   B. won't have
   C. shouldn't have
   D. couldn't have

6. I have seen one of Grant Wood's paintings in a museum, but I _____ .
   A. from where can't remember
   B. where can't remember
   C. can't remember from where
   D. can't remember where

7. I'm glad you _____ me that you had already completed the report.
   A. had told
   B. told
   C. were telling
   D. tell

8. That presentation was far too advanced _____ as an introductory lecture.
   A. to be suiting
   B. for suiting
   C. to be suitable
   D. suitably

9. He is _____ his three brothers.
   A. taller of
   B. the tallest
   C. taller than
   D. tallest of

10. I really regret _____ harder to increase my savings.
    A. not having tried
    B. not to try
    C. not to tried
    D. not to trying

11. He _____ me to repeat something four times yesterday.
    A. had asked
    B. asked
    C. has been asking
    D. had been asking

12. We couldn't have completed the project without Ahmed, who _____ a great deal of expertise to the team.
    A. brought
    B. had brought
    C. will have brought
    D. will be bringing

13. Once he _____ that he wasn't going to be able to go to college, he felt a lot better.
    A. accepts
    B. did accept
    C. will accept
    D. had accepted

14. She was upset about not receiving an invitation; we _____ have invited her.
    A. must
    B. may
    C. should
    D. ought

15. Your monetary compensation agreement is in the envelope _____ was forwarded to your attorney.
    A. which
    B. in which
    C. where
    D. in that

GRAMMAR REVIEW EXERCISES – SET 3

1. I expect her _____ out of her parents' house now that she has finished college.
   A. to move
   B. moving
   C. being moved
   D. to have been moving

2. This isn't my first draft of the assignment; I _____ it.
   A. had yet re-written
   B. re-wrote already
   C. have already re-written
   D. re-written already

3. He's getting married tomorrow, and _____ him so worried.
   A. never have I seen
   B. never I saw
   C. I have seen never
   D. I saw never

4. Perhaps she _____ stay home than go shopping with us.
   A. might better
   B. would rather
   C. much better
   D. could rather

5. He gets _____ grades of all the students in his class.
   A. the best
   B. the better
   C. the best of
   D. better than

6. Just after we _____ , he decided to leave.
   A. had arrived
   B. have arrived
   C. are arriving
   D. were arrived

7. The teacher told me off _____ to class.
   A. to be late
   B. to being late
   C. for being late
   D. being late

8. I'm sure that _____ to Disneyland will be a lot of fun.
   A. to go
   B. going
   C. to be going
   D. having gone

9. In addition to _____ , Susan also does knitting.
   A. sew
   B. she sews
   C. sewing
   D. she sewing

10. My new job is going well now that I have gotten used _____ so early.
    A. to getting up
    B. getting up
    C. to get up
    D. get up

11. _____ my best friend only once since she moved to Minneapolis.
    A. I have seen
    B. Did I see
    C. Have I seen
    D. I saw

12. The doctor advised me to do something that I never would have thought _____.
    A. to be done
    B. to do
    C. to doing
    D. of doing

13. It was time John _____ the situation.
    A. accept
    B. accepted
    C. accepts
    D. was accepting

14. The new supermarket is believed _____ next week.
    A. be closing
    B. to be closing
    C. it is closing
    D. to having its closing

15. That problem is between you and _____; you shouldn't discuss it with anyone else.
    A. I
    B. me
    C. mine
    D. my

PART 2 – MET READING TIPS AND EXERCISES

Strategies and Tips for the MET Reading Test

The MET reading test contains thirty questions. You will see two long passages and two sets of three excerpts on this part of the exam.

There will be 5 questions on each of the long passages.

There will be 10 questions on each set of excerpts.

In order to do your best on this section of the test, you will need tips and strategies in order to work quickly and to help manage the time.

The biggest piece of advice that you need for the reading test is as follows:

> Be sure to look at the questions for each passage BEFORE reading the passage itself. This will help you anticipate what to look for as you read the paragraphs.

You also need to know which types of questions you will see on the MET reading test, so that you can learn how to answer each one.

There are five types of questions on the MET reading test:

1. Main idea questions
2. Specific detail questions
3. Implication and inference questions
4. Vocabulary in context questions
5. Questions on the author's purpose or opinion

Bearing the above advice in mind, you should now go to the next section for specific strategies for each type of question that you will encounter on the MET reading test.

TIPS FOR MAIN IDEA QUESTIONS

- For these types of questions, you have to ignore answer choices that give specific points mentioned in the passage.
- For main idea questions, you have to determine the overall point of the passage.
- To answer these types of questions correctly, you should identify the thesis statement of the reading passage.
- Remember that the thesis statement explains the main point of the passage.
- The thesis statement is normally included in the first paragraph of the passage, and it is very often the first or last sentence of the first paragraph.
- The incorrect answer choices will contain some specific details from the passage, but for this type of question think generally, instead of getting distracted by specific points.

Now try the sample main idea question below. The answer is on the next page.

A true feat of modern engineering, the Alaska Highway was constructed to link Edmonton in Alberta, Canada, to Fairbanks, Alaska. The first step in completing the mammoth project was to plan the exact route that the road was going to take. Ground and aerial surveys were conducted only slightly in advance of the construction of the road, with the survey teams working just miles ahead of the construction crew in some cases. Apart from the challenges inherent in building a road in such inclement conditions, bridges had to be erected and culverts had to be laid in drainage ditches. Swampland along the route was a further complication, and efforts to avoid the waterlogged ground created many bends in the road.

1. The main idea of this passage is that:
    A. The construction of the Alaska Highway was hampered by inclement weather.
    B. Many difficulties surrounded getting permission to build the Alaska Highway.
    C. The construction of the Alaska Highway was an impressive achievement.
    D. The construction of major highways usually involves ground and road surveys.

Answer: The passage is stating that the construction of the Alaska Highway was an impressive achievement. We know this because of the word "feat" in the first sentence, as well as the words "inherent challenges" and "complication" later in the passage. You may be tempted to choose answer B, but the passage focuses on the construction of the road, not the permission. Answers A and D are incorrect because they are too specific. So, the correct answer is C.

TIPS FOR SPECIFIC DETAIL QUESTIONS

- For specific detail questions, you have to ignore answers that are too general.
- Therefore, be sure you choose a specific answer.
- In other words, you should ignore answer choices that cover the main idea of the passage or that give general information.
- Specific detail questions sometimes begin with the phrases "according to the passage" or "the passage states that."
- Questions in this category rely on your ability to search through the passage and find a specific piece of information.
- The distractor answers will be of three types:
    a) specific information that does not answer the question
    b) information that is too general
    c) answers that seem correct but which are not directly stated in the text

Now try the sample specific detail questions below.

Gibberellins are a complex group of plant hormones that are involved in many botanical processes. Commonly used in combination with similar botanical hormones called auxins, their primary function is to promote plant growth by controlling the elongation of cells. They also promote the formation of fruit and seed, as well as delay aging in leaves. Having become important for commercial reasons in recent years, the hormones are also used to help meet the ever-growing demand for new hybrids of plants and flowers.

2. Which of the following best describes the botanical significance of gibberellins?
    A. Without them, plant hormones would be involved in more processes.
    B. Because of gibberellins, plants cells enlarge, thereby causing plants to grow.
    C. Leaves age more quickly, owing to the function of gibberellins.
    D. Gibberellins have nocuous consequences for fruits and seeds.

Answer: Gibberellins are of botanical significance because they cause plants cells to enlarge, thereby causing plants to grow. The passage states that the primary function of gibberellins "is to promote plant growth by controlling the elongation of cells." The other answer choices are not supported by the passage. So, the correct answer is B.

Now try another type of specific detail question.

According to Stephen Krashen's input hypothesis, a language learner improves his or her language skills when he or she is exposed to language input such as lectures or reading materials that are one level above the learner's current level of language ability. The learner's language output, such as verbal or written expressions, is not seen to have any direct correlation to his or her actual learning ability.

3. Which of the following statements is supported by the passage?
    A. Spoken language reflects the learner's real skills.
    B. Learners can best improve their language skills when their learning is appropriately challenging.
    C. Traditional grammatical skills are very important for language learning.
    D. Writing output is related to language learning.

Answer: Answers A and D are contradicted by the last sentence of the passage. Grammatical skills are not even mentioned in the passage, so answer C is not supported by the passage. Answer B is supported by the statement that lectures or reading materials should be "one level above the learner's current level of language ability." So, you need to choose answer is B.

TIPS FOR IMPLICATION AND INFERENCE QUESTIONS

- Interpretation questions may be of two types: (1) The question may ask you what the passage implies or what can be inferred from the passage. (2) The question may ask you to make an assumption or to draw a conclusion.
- "Imply" means to suggest something without stating it directly.
- Inference or interpretation questions ask you to read between the lines of the passage and draw conclusions.
- Inference or implication questions sometimes begin with the phrases "the passage implies" or "it can be inferred from the passage that."
- The word "suggests" is sometimes substituted for "implies."
- Remember that these questions are asking you to make only a very small logical conclusion based upon information that is clearly stated in the passage.
- So, you will need to find the specific sentence in the passage that provides the basis for the conclusion given in the correct answer choice.
- Incorrect answer choices will require significant assumptions or "wild guesses."

Now try the sample implication and inference questions below.

Research shows that the rise in teenage smoking over the last ten years took place primarily in youth from more affluent families, in other words, families in which both parents were working and earning good incomes. Therefore, these teenagers were not from disadvantaged homes, as most people seemed to believe. The facts demonstrate quite the opposite because the most striking and precipitous rise in smoking has been for teenagers from the most financially advantaged backgrounds. Furthermore, because of various lawsuits against the major tobacco companies, the price of cigarettes has actually declined sharply over the past decade. The paradox is that the increased demand for cigarettes originated from new teenage smokers who were from well-off families. Yet, contrary to these market forces, the price of tobacco products fell during this time.

4. Which of the following can be inferred from the passage?
    A. The majority of new teenage smokers years could have afforded to pay higher prices for tobacco.
    B. Parents of affluent families are often not aware of the smoking habits of their children.
    C. Smoking among teenagers from disadvantaged homes also increased during the past decade.
    D. Major tobacco companies have recently faced bankruptcy.

Now try the other sample implication and inference question.

5. From the information in the passage, it is reasonable to assume that:
    A. teenagers from affluent families smoke more than teenagers from disadvantaged homes.
    B. the price of tobacco products is normally unrelated to market forces.
    C. the price of cigarettes has fallen more than expected during the last ten years.
    D. increased demand for a product can cause its price to go up.

Answer (Question 4): Look for words and phrases in the passage that express the writer's viewpoint. See the phrase "contrary to these market forces" in the last sentence of the passage. The market forces refer to the factors that would have caused the price of tobacco to increase. Based on the word "contrary," it seems safe to conclude that the majority of new teenage smokers could have afforded to pay higher prices for tobacco, but in spite of this fact, the price of tobacco did not go up. So, the correct answer is A.

Answer (Question 5): The passage states that the price of tobacco should have gone up because youngsters from wealthy families could have afforded to pay a higher price. The following statement is the best assumption to draw from the passage because it generalizes this aspect of the pricing: "increased demand for a product can cause its price to go up." So, answer D is the most accurate assumption.

TIPS FOR VOCABULARY QUESTIONS

- The question will ask you to interpret the meaning of a word or phrase from the passage.
- Very carefully re-read the sentence in the passage that contains required the word or phrase.
- Look for synonyms in the passage that may be similar in meaning to the unknown word or phrase.

Now look at the passage again and try the sample vocabulary question.

Research shows that the rise in teenage smoking over the last ten years took place primarily in youth from more affluent families, in other words, families in which both parents were working and earning good incomes. Therefore, these teenagers were not from disadvantaged homes, as most people seemed to believe. The facts demonstrate quite the opposite because the most striking and ***precipitous*** rise in smoking has been for teenagers from the most financially advantageous backgrounds. Furthermore, because of various lawsuits against the major tobacco companies, the price of cigarettes has actually declined sharply over the past decade. The paradox is that the increased demand for cigarettes originated from new teenage smokers who were from well-off families. Yet, contrary to these market forces, the price of tobacco products fell during this time.

6. Which of the following is the best meaning of the word ***precipitous*** as it is used in this passage?
   A. dramatic
   B. unbelievable
   C. predictable
   D. dangerous

Answer: Look for other words in the passage that are synonyms for the word in the question. "Dramatic" and "precipitous" are synonyms in the context of this passage. The word "striking" from the passage is also a synonym for "precipitous." So, the correct answer is A.

TIPS FOR QUESTIONS ON THE AUTHOR

- The question may ask you to determine the purpose of the author or of the passage.
- The question may ask you about the author's tone, attitude, opinions, or assumptions.
- For these types of questions, you first need to consider the tone and style of the passage.
- To determine the tone, look for opinion words in the passage such as "best" or "most important."
- Then make a logical conclusion about the author's opinion or purpose based on the tone and style.

Now try the sample questions below.

"All knowledge that is about human society, and not about the natural world, is historical knowledge, and therefore rests upon judgment and interpretation. This is not to say that facts or data are non-existent, but that facts get their importance from what is made of them in interpretation, for interpretations depend very much on who the interpreter is, who he or she is addressing, what his or her purpose is, and at what historical moment the interpretation takes place" (Excerpt from *Culture and Imperialism,* Edward Said).

7. The author's primary purpose is to:
   A. assert that historical knowledge diverges from knowledge about nature.
   B. emphasize the historical significance of facts and data.
   C. argue that historical knowledge hinges on analyses and opinions.
   D. point out that historical knowledge is dubious from an academic perspective.

Answer: In the first sentence, the author states that "historical knowledge . . . rests upon judgment and interpretation . . . Facts get their importance from what is made of them in interpretation." Interpretation is based on how something is analyzed, as well as the opinion of the interpreter. So, the correct answer is C.

Now try the other sample question.

In Southern Spain and France, Stone Age artists painted stunning drawings on the walls of caves nearly 30,000 years ago. Painting pictures of the animals upon which they relied for food, the artists worked by the faint light of lamps that were made of animal fat and twigs. In addition to having to work in relative darkness, the artists had to endure great physical discomfort since the inner chambers of the caves were sometimes less than three feet in height. Thus, the artists were required to crouch or squat uncomfortably as they practiced their craft.

8. Which of the following best expresses the attitude of the writer?
   A. It is surprising that the tools of Stone Age artists were similar to those that artists use today.
   B. It is amazing that Stone Age artists were able to paint such beautiful creations in spite of the extreme conditions they faced.
   C. The lack of light in the caves had an effect on their esthetic quality.
   D. It is predictable that Stone Age artists would paint pictures of animals.

Answer: The attitude of the writer is that it is amazing that Stone Age artists were able to paint such beautiful creations in spite of the extreme conditions they faced. For questions like this one, look for adjectives in the passage that give hints about the author's point of view. The phrase "stunning drawings" indicates the author's amazement. So, the correct answer is B.

Now try the practice reading tests in the next section.

PART 3 – MET READING AND GRAMMAR PRACTICE TESTS

MET READING AND GRAMMAR PRACTICE TEST 1

There are 50 total questions in this practice test, just like the real exam. You will be allowed 65 minutes to complete the real reading and grammar test, so you should take an hour and 5 minutes to complete each practice test in order to simulate exam conditions. Choose one answer from the choices provided. On the real test, you will need to put your answers on a separate answer sheet.

GRAMMAR

1. I have no idea where I put my jacket. It could be _____.
    A. anywhere
    B. elsewhere
    C. somewhere else
    D. other place

2. The remodeling on the upstairs of our house is _____ finished.
    A. soon
    B. almost
    C. near
    D. far

3. Although he was extremely careful driving the car, he _____ an accident.
    A. did
    B. has
    C. do have
    D. did have

4. You can put that bag on the seat between you and _____ .
    A. I
    B. me
    C. mine
    D. my

5. Many people like going for long walks in the park, but _____ do not.
    A. another
    B. other
    C. others
    D. some other

6. That new student, _____ remember, is supposed to be very intelligent.
   A. whose name I can't
   B. which name I can't
   C. that I can't name
   D. whom I can't name

7. There were many casualties in the area, even though the weather report said that _____ prepared for the tornado.
   A. people should
   B. people should have
   C. people ought have
   D. ought people have

8. At 6'4" Jane is the _____ four sisters.
   A. tallest of the
   B. taller of her
   C. taller than her
   D. most tall of the

9. Sarah told everyone my secret, but _____ we are still good friends.
   A. furthermore
   B. despite of that
   C. contrarily
   D. in spite of that

10. I would have bought that new dress _____ more money.
    A. did I have
    B. have I have
    C. if I did have
    D. had I had

11. I finally decided _____ New College after I got confirmation of my scholarship.
    A. to attend
    B. to attend to
    C. attending
    D. to attend at

12. He got _____ cheating on the exam.
    A. down on
    B. through
    C. away with
    D. up to

13. We arrived at a solution that can _____ .
    A. be easy achieved
    B. be easily achieved
    C. easy to be achieved
    D. easily to be achieved

14. He is so shy that not a word _____ during the meeting yesterday.
    A. he did say
    B. was he saying
    C. did he say
    D. was it said

15. Our business is going quite well now that we have acquired all _____ we need to sell.
    A. to the merchandise
    B. of the merchandise
    C. for the merchandise
    D. of merchandise

16. After the fire last week, the all of the paintings in the museum are believed _____ .
    A. to have been destroyed
    B. destroying
    C. that are destroyed
    D. to destroy

17. My grandma is coming to visit me _____ the beginning of the month.
    A. in
    B. at
    C. on
    D within

18. If you hadn't eaten so much, you _____ a stomach ache.
    A. might not have gotten
    B. ought not to have gotten
    C. might have gotten
    D. could get

19. _____ book is the best one I've read so far.
    A. Those
    B. This
    C. Their's
    D. These

20. You're a fool if you believe her because she has told those lies and many _____ .
    A. other
    B. another
    C. others
    D. anothers

READING

This passage is about tornadoes.

Although improved weather observation practices seem to have reduced the severity of tornadoes in recent years, they continue to be one of the most severe types of weather-related events. While many people live in fear of tornadoes and the path of destruction they wreak, very few understand the facts behind these weather events. Even fewer people are aware of how to protect themselves and their property if a tornado were to strike.

Although having **myriad** sizes and shapes, tornadoes can be classified as weak, strong, or violent. It is notable that the majority of all tornadoes are categorized as weak. To be classified as a weak tornado, the duration of the event must be less than ten minutes and the speed must be under 110 miles per hour. Strong tornadoes, which comprise approximately ten percent of all twisters, may have durations of more than twenty minutes each and speeds of up to 205 miles per hour. Violent tornadoes are the rarest since they occur less than one percent of the time. Although uncommon, violent tornadoes last for more than one hour and result in the greatest loss of life. While a violent tornado can destroy a solidly-constructed, well-built home, weak tornadoes can also cause a great deal of damage.

Because tornadoes have serious consequences for communities and their inhabitants, safety measures are of the utmost importance during severe weather conditions. To protect themselves, residents should go to the basement their homes. If the house has no basement, a person should find the lowest floor of a nearby building and position him or herself under a heavy object. If no building is located nearby, a person stuck in a tornado can lie prostrate in a nearby ditch or other low area of land and protect his or her head.

21. What is the passage mainly about?
    A. the yearly number of deaths from tornadoes
    B. the various speeds of tornadoes
    C. providing residents with facts about tornadoes
    D. how to classify tornadoes and protect against them

22. In the first sentence of paragraph 2, what does the word **myriad** mean?
    A. limited
    B. extreme
    C. many
    D. average

23. In paragraph 2, what is the author's main purpose?
    A. to explain how tornadoes are categorized
    B. to identify the most frequent type of tornadoes
    C. to emphasize the loss of life and damage to property caused by tornadoes
    D. to compare weak tornadoes to strong tornadoes

24. What is the safest place to be when a tornado strikes?
    A. a ditch
    B. a low area of land
    C. the underground floor of a building
    D. under a piece of sturdy furniture

25. In the author's opinion, tornadoes are considered to be a severe weather phenomenon because:
    A. many people fear them.
    B. of their different shapes and sizes.
    C. they can be placed into three discrete categories.
    D. they can result in death and devastation.

This passage is about Mount Rushmore.

In the Black Hills in the state of South Dakota, four visages protrude from the side of a mountain. The faces are those of four United States' presidents: George Washington, Thomas Jefferson, Theodore Roosevelt, and Abraham Lincoln. Overseen and directed by the Danish-American sculptor John Gutzon Borglum, the work on this giant display of outdoor art was a Herculean task that took fourteen years to complete.

A South Dakota state historian named Doane Robinson originally conceived of the idea for the memorial sculpture. He proposed that the work be dedicated to popular figures who were prominent in the western United States and accordingly suggested statues of popular western heroes such as Buffalo Bill Cody and Kit Carson. Deeming a project dedicated to popular heroes **frivolous**, Borglum rejected Robinson's proposal. It was Borglum's firm conviction that the mountain carving be used to memorialize individuals of national rather than regional importance.

Mount Rushmore therefore became a national memorial dedicated to the four presidents who were considered most pivotal in United States' history. Washington was chosen on the basis of being the first president. Jefferson, who was of course a president, was also instrumental in the writing of the Declaration of Independence. Lincoln was selected on the basis of the mettle he demonstrated during the American Civil War and Roosevelt for his development of Square Deal policy, as well as for being a proponent of the construction of the Panama Canal.

Commencing with Washington's head first, Borglum quickly realized that it would be best to work on only one head at a time, in order to make each one compatible with its surroundings. To help him visualize the final outcome, he fashioned a 1.5-meter-high plaster model on a scale of 1 to 12.

Work on the venture began in 1927 and was completed in 1941. The cost of the project was nearly $1,000,000, which would be worth over $70 million dollars today. The financing for the project was provided mainly from national government funds, but some charitable donations also came in from members of the public.

26. In the third sentence of paragraph 2, what does the word **frivolous** mean?
    A. unimportant
    B. serious
    C. expensive
    D. unwanted

27. According to the passage, why did Doane Robinson suggest that western heroes be the subject of the monument?
   A. Western heroes were well-known and loved by the public.
   B. The westward expansion movement would not have been successful without Buffalo Bill Cody and Kit Carson.
   C. Such figures were of national significance.
   D. The dedication of a sculpture to Western heroes would raise their profiles.

28. What is the purpose of paragraph 3?
   A. to mention that there was some debate about which presidents to choose
   B. to show that these presidents were chosen because they changed United States' policy and history
   C. to explain that these presidents were well known internationally
   D. to emphasize that these presidents were chosen since they were of some importance regionally

29. Why does the author go into detail about Borglum and his working practices?
   A. to imply that he was a talented and perceptive artist
   B. to criticize him for being profligate in his spending for the Mount Rushmore project
   C. to suggest that his work was misunderstood during his lifetime
   D. to demonstrate that he was an incompetent craftsman

30. According to the passage, which of the following is true about Mount Rushmore's funding?
   A. Private individuals contributed most of the financial backing for the work.
   B. It was paid for over a 14-year time period.
   C. It cost millions of dollars in funding.
   D. The project was predominantly paid for on a federal level.

A) Visit Seatown Aquarium

Learn All About Your Fish Friends.

The Seatown Aquarium will have its Grand Reopening to the public on May 25.

Visit anytime from the Grand Reopening until June 25th and any children you accompany can enter for half-price when you present this coupon.

NOTE: Limited to one offer per group. May not be used in conjunction with any other offer. The discount is not valid on Memorial Day Weekend. This coupon has no monetary value.

B) Fish Facts

All fish have two common traits: they live in water and they have a spine. So, all fish are vertebrates. Yet, the various species of fish can differ dramatically from each another.

Some fish have fins, gills, and scales, and they reproduce by laying eggs. In contrast, eels have bodies like snakes. Sharks, the largest types of fish, give birth to their young and eat tiny fish. Other species, like the seahorse, are so bizarre they almost seem other-worldly.

One reason sea life is so varied is because water covers over seventy percent of our planet. Fish live in a variety of places, from coral reefs to streams, rivers, and the ocean. Another factor is that fish are unique on the evolutionary scale. Over time, fish have developed special senses. Fish rely less on their vision and more on their hearing, taste, and smell. Fossils reveal that they have been on the planet for more than 500 million years. There are more than 32,000 living fish species, which is greater than the total of all other vertebrate species combined.

C) Why Animals Are the Best Athletes

Studies of the human body show that performance ability can be enhanced by regular strenuous training exercises. Some human athletic records may seem unbeatable, but these achievements require great effort. When compared to the innate abilities of animals, the athletic training and performance of human beings seem unimpressive, paling in comparison to the phenomenal feats performed naturally by members of the animal kingdom.

Whales, for example, usually dive to 3,700 feet below sea level. However, the human body can withstand underwater depths up to only 2,300 feet, and even attempting to do so would require special equipment.

Human performance also seems paltry in swimming when compared to other species. The human record for the fastest swimming speed is 5.3 miles per hour. However, the sailfish averages a speed of 68 miles per hour, and the penguin, which is not even a member of the fish species, can flutter across the surface of the water as fast as 22 miles per hour.

The following questions refer to section A.

31. What can be inferred about Seatown Aquarium?
    A. It often offers coupons to the public.
    B. It usually allows only one coupon per group.
    C. It has been closed for a certain time period recently.
    D. It is closed on Memorial Day Weekend.

32. What should someone who wants to visit with their children for half-price do?
    A. Go to the aquarium on May 25.
    B. Have the children accompany them on June 25.
    C. Use the coupon with another offer from the aquarium.
    D. Bring the coupon with them when they visit the aquarium.

The following questions refer to section B.

33. What characteristic do all fish have in common?
    A. They give birth to their young.
    B. They all have a backbone.
    C. They have fins, gills, and scales.
    D. They eat other tiny fish.

34. What does the author mention about the seahorse?
    A. It has a very unusual appearance.
    B. It reproduces by laying eggs.
    C. It has poor vision.
    D. It lives in coral reefs.

35. According to the passage, how have fish evolved?
    A. They have reproduced more than 32,000 times.
    B. They have adapted by having some heightened senses.
    C. They have poor senses of hearing, taste, and smell.
    D. They have become imbedded in fossils on our planet.

The following questions refer to section C.

36. What is the main idea of the passage?
    A. The human body needs training in order to compete in athletic events.
    B. Fish can swim far better than human beings.
    C. Fish can go deeper under water than humans can.
    D. The athletic performance of some animals is superior to that of humans.

37. According to the passage, why do people sometimes need special diving equipment?
    A. The human body is not designed to cope underwater like fish can.
    B. It is only needed when diving more than 2,300 feet underwater.
    C. It can only be used to depths of up to 3,700 feet.
    D. Because they cannot swim fast enough.

38. Why does the author mention penguins?
    A. to describe how fish can flutter
    B. to compare their movement to that of fish
    C. to criticize how they cause damage to the ocean
    D. to point out a surprising fact

39. How does the author feel about the athletic performance of animals?
    A. It requires further research.
    B. It is remarkable and extraordinary.
    C. It should be more impressive.
    D. Some fish should be able to dive to deeper levels.

The following question refers to two or more sections.

40. With what statement would the author of section B agree most strongly?
    A. People should visit aquariums more often.
    B. Whales are the most outstanding of the fish species.
    C. Animal performance has developed because of evolution.
    D. People should study more facts about the athletic performance of fish.

A) Coffee Tasting at Newton Cafe

It's Coffee Time!

Learn the difference between Columbian and Costa Rican! Get free espresso or latte!

Try different coffee flavor sensations at our free coffee tasting session.

You will learn about different types of coffee based upon your tastes and preferences.

First, sample coffee from different countries around the world to see which one you like best. Then put in an order to get your favorite brew for free.

We use only the very best, high quality coffee beans from fair trade organizations.

B) Bad News for Coffee Drinkers

Recent studies show that coffee may be even worse for us than we thought. We have known for a few years now that coffee can elevate blood pressure and also lead to high cholesterol, but new research has revealed a whole host of other health problems caused by the beverage.

If you frequently suffer from stomach ache, it would be a good idea to cut down on coffee or stop drinking it altogether. A new study demonstrates that coffee stimulates the secretion of gastric acid, which can lead to stomach upset.

Consuming coffee later in the day is strongly linked to insomnia, which can cause more health problems like anxiety and depression. Caffeine stays in your system for six hours, so don't have coffee after 2:00 pm unless you drink decaffeinated.

A further study has shown that coffee changes our sense of taste, making sweet things seem less sweet. **This** may cause us to crave more sweets. However, avoid adding sugar, cream, or milk to your coffee. With raised calorie levels, continued consumption of such sugar-laden beverages can lead to obesity and type-two diabetes.

C) What is Fair Trade Coffee?

Farming and trade organizations have created what is known as fair trade coffee. Based on a cooperative farming approach, coffee farmers must pay certification fees to take part in the scheme. Farmers receive a price per pound for their coffee beans after harvesting them. The certification fees are deducted first, and from the remaining amount, ten cents per pound goes to marketing and advertising costs, and twenty cents per pound is taken for local projects and education.

Fair trade organizations have been established with the best intentions in an attempt to educate and empower farmers to earn a decent wage from their work. However, unintended fair trade issues affect the consumer, as well as the farmer.

To understand how the fair trade coffee system functions, first we need to look the different prices growers can get for their product. The coffee market for farmers is divided into different categories based on quality and price, from the lowest quality, which is called standard grade, to the highest quality, known as specialty grade.

Coffee beans sold as fair trade can come from any quality category of coffee, so farmers use lower quality coffee as fair trade, which causes quality for coffee drinkers to suffer. Farmers end up selling their higher-grade coffees on the open market, out of the fair trade system, because they can get a much higher price for this product due to its better quality.

The outcome is that the well-intentioned consumer who buys fair trade beans gets a low-quality product with poor flavor. This causes an unsatisfactory experience for the consumer and undermines the effort of the farmer and fair trade organizations.

The following questions refer to section A.

41. What is the main purpose of this text?
    A. to introduce facts about coffee
    B. to explain how coffee is classified
    C. to give tips about coffee
    D. to describe an offer

The following questions refer to section B.

42. What does the author mention about high cholesterol?
    A. It leads to gastric acid.
    B. It can be caused by drinking coffee.
    C. It results only from drinking coffee.
    D. It is linked to high blood pressure.

43. According to the passage, how can coffee cause stomach ache?
    A. Drinking too much of it fills up the stomach.
    B. The caffeine in the beverage irritates the stomach.
    C. It makes acidity levels in the stomach higher.
    D. Stomach ache is linked to adding too much sugar.

44. Why does the author mention anxiety and depression?
    A. to exemplify another problem caused by drinking too much coffee
    B. to demonstrate that caffeine remains in the human body for several hours
    C. to illustrate how caffeine is related to insomnia
    D. to criticize coffee drinkers for overindulging in the beverage

45. In the last paragraph, what fact does **This** refer to?
    A. sweet things taste less sweet
    B. a further study
    C. avoiding sugar, cream, or milk
    D. craving more sweets

The following questions refer to section C.

46. What is the main purpose of the article?
    A. to describe where fair trade coffee comes from and how it is classified
    B. to discuss fair trade coffee pricing, classification, and consumer outcomes
    C. to explain how the fair trade coffee system functions
    D. to talk about how fair trade coffee affects the consumer

47. Why does the author mention certification fees and prices?
    A. to explain the costs and problems for farmers
    B. to show how pricing is related to classification
    C. to elucidate the classification process
    D. to demonstrate how these aspects are related to harvesting

48. According to the passage, how is fair trade related to coffee quality?
    A. Fair trade organizations are responsible for specialty grade coffee.
    B. Classification has had a negative effect on fair trade coffee quality.
    C. Dividing coffee into quality categories negatively affects the open market.
    D. Farmers have become confused about where to sell their product.

49. How does the author feel about fair trade coffee?
    A. It was created with poor objectives.
    B. It should be better governed by farmers.
    C. Its production should be increased in the future.
    D. It has had some unfortunate and unexpected outcomes.

The following question refers to two or more sections.

50. What is a negative aspect of coffee production and consumption?
    A. It has become too expensive and complicated lately.
    B. Its quality and production have diminished in recent years.
    C. It can cause issues for consumers and farmers.
    D. It can lead to problems with the environment.

MET READING AND GRAMMAR PRACTICE TEST 2

There are 50 total questions in this practice test, just like the real exam. You will be allowed 65 minutes to complete the real reading and grammar test, so you should take an hour and 5 minutes to complete each practice test in order to simulate exam conditions. Choose one answer from the choices provided. On the real test, you will need to put your answers on a separate answer sheet.

GRAMMAR

1. She is such a nervous person that very rarely _____ relaxed.
   A. she appears
   B. she is appearing
   C. does she appear
   D. she does appear

2. The paper is in the cabinet _____ we use to store the pens and pencils.
   A. that
   B. there
   C. where
   D. in which

3. Starting a new business involves sizing _____ the competition.
   A. in
   B. under
   C. up
   D. over

4. We hope _____ on vacation on Saturday.
   A. to go
   B. to going
   C. going
   D. to have been going

5. No sooner _____ at the party than Sung Li came in.
   A. we arrived
   B. we had arrived
   C. had we arrived
   D. we were arriving

6. Alison is at home recovering _____ the _____ flu.
   A. with
   B. to
   C. for
   D. from

7. She wouldn't have gotten fired _____ honest.
   A. she was
   B. had she been
   C. was she
   D. she had been

8. That was a pretty good movie, but I prefer the one _____ .
   A. to which I saw last week
   B. I saw last week
   C. which last week I saw
   D. I saw it last week

9. I requested that my friend _____ to the party.
   A. to be invited
   B. be inviting
   C. to have been invited
   D. be invited

10. Iced tea on a hot summer day is one of life's _____ pleasures.
    A. greater
    B. most great
    C. greatest
    D. the greatest

11. That form was compulsory, so _____ it in.
    A. you should have filled
    B. should you have filled
    C. should have you filled
    D. you should filled

12. I don't want to eat at McDonalds. I would rather eat _____ .
    A. anyplace
    B. somewhere else
    C. somewhere
    D. other place

13. _____ students here study a lot and work hard.
    A. Almost
    B. Most of
    C. Almost of
    D. Most

14. The suspects were interrogated, but all of them denied _____ the car.
    A. stealing
    B. to steal
    C. to stealing
    D. to have stolen

15. Although some people can't stand our boss, I can put _____ her sometimes.
    A. down
    B. in for
    C. up with
    D. off

16. _____ my exam today, I wanted to get a good night's sleep last night.
    A. While I have
    B. Because of
    C. While having
    D. Because having

17. She has many _____ hobbies apart from fitness and hiking.
    A. other
    B. another
    C. others
    D. more of

18. I know you are normally very careful, but you _____ to be extra cautious when you travel.
    A. did need
    B. do need
    C. have needed
    D. did

19. Although I will leave this job tomorrow, I feel so happy _____ with such wonderful people.
    A. to have
    B. to have worked
    C. to have been worked
    D. worked

20. Even though the three of you have argued, _____ shouldn't have hard feelings against her.
    A. you and he
    B. you and him
    C. him and you
    D. yours and his

READING

This passage is about two famous people.

Sir Isaac Newton and Albert Einstein were certainly two of the most influential scientific thinkers of all time. In his first mathematical formulation of gravity, published in 1687, Newton posited that the same force that kept the moon from being propelled away from the earth also applied to gravity at the earth's surface. While this finding, termed the Law of Universal Gravitation, is said to have been occasioned by Newton's observation of the fall of an apple from a tree in the orchard at his home, in reality the idea did not come to the scientist in **a flash of inspiration,** but was developed slowly over time.

It is because of Newton's work that we currently understand the effect of gravity on the earth as a global system. As a result of Newton's investigation into the subject of gravity, we know today that geological features such as mountains and canyons can cause variances in the earth's gravitational force. Newton must also be acknowledged for the realization that the force of gravity becomes less robust as the distance from the equator diminishes, due to the rotation of the earth, as well as the declining mass and density of the planet from the equator to the poles.

Yet, throughout his lifetime, Newton remained perplexed about the causes of the power implicit in the variables of his mathematical equations on gravity. In other words, he was unable adequately to explain the natural forces upon which the power of gravity relied. Even though he tried to justify these forces by describing them merely as phenomena of nature, differing hypotheses on these phenomena still abound today.

In 1915, Einstein addressed Newton's reservations by developing the revolutionary theory of general relativity. Einstein asserted that the paths of objects in motion can sometimes deviate or change direction over the course of time as a result of the curvature of space time. Numerous subsequent investigations into and tests of the theory of general relativity have unequivocally supported Einstein's groundbreaking work.

21. What is the author's main purpose?
    A. to analyze natural phenomena
    B. to emphasize Newton's and Einstein's achievements
    C. to criticize various gravitational theories
    D. to give background about Newton's life

22. In the last sentence of paragraph 1, what does the phrase **a flash of inspiration** mean?
    A. in hindsight
    B. with trepidation
    C. all of a sudden
    D. with clarity

23. According to the passage, which of the following is a factor in the diminishment of the force of gravity when one is closer to the equator?
    A. Because the relative weight of the Earth is higher in this particular geographical location
    B. Because the Earth's gravitational force has changed positions
    C. Because one is further from geographical features such as mountains and canyons
    D. Because the Earth rotates in a different way near the equator

24. What is the main idea of paragraph 3 of this passage?
    A. Newton developed conflicting scientific hypotheses.
    B. Newton had a research question that he could not answer.
    C. Newton extensively analyzed natural phenomena.
    D. Newton was often perplexed and usually felt inadequate.

25. Why does the author mention that Einstein's work has been "unequivocally supported" in the last paragraph?
    A. to indicate how Einstein's work was supported by that of Newton
    B. to explain the paths of objects in motion
    C. to suggest that this theory may change in the future
    D. to show that Einstein's ideas were somewhat ahead of their time

This passage is about archeology.

The discipline of archeology has been developing since wealthy Europeans began to plunder relics from distant lands in the early nineteenth century. Initially considered an upper-class hobby, archeology in general and archeological field methods in particular have undergone many developments and experienced many challenges in recent years.

Before the field excavation begins, a viable site must first be located. A logical locality to begin searching is one near a site in which artifacts have been found previously. Failing that, an archeologist must consider, at a minimum, whether the potential site would have been habitable for people in antiquity.

Once the site has been located, the ground is surveyed and pits are dug. The excavation, which is a meticulous and lengthy process, then begins. Since variations in soil composition can be used to identify changes in climate and living conditions, the walls of the pit must be kept uniformly straight as the dig progresses.

The soil that is removed from the pit is sifted through a sieve or similar device, consisting of a screen that is suspended across a metal or wooden frame. After the soil is placed in the sieve, the archaeologist gently **oscillates** the device. As the mechanism goes back and forth in this way, the soil falls to the ground below, while larger objects are caught in the mesh. Throughout this process, all findings are entered in a written record to ensure that every artifact is cataloged.

Finally, the arduous task of interpreting the findings ensues. During the last three centuries, various approaches have been utilized in this respect. Throughout the early 1800s, most fossil recovery took place on the European continent, resulting in an extremely Euro-centric method of examination and dissemination of findings. Lamentably, the misapprehension that the *homo sapiens* species was European in origin began to take shape both in the archeological and wider communities at that time.

26. What is the passage mainly about?
    A. Modern archeological methods are methodical and time-consuming.
    B. Protruding artifacts can create difficulties during excavation.
    C. An archeologist has many things to consider when selecting a site.
    D. Preparing written archeological records is tedious.

27. The word **oscillates** in this passage is closest in meaning to:
    A. moves
    B. sways
    C. attaches
    D. manipulates

28. According to the passage, what do archeologists consider when choosing a potential site for excavation?
    A. whether research can be conducted on the site
    B. whether electricity is presently available
    C. whether the site existed in pre-historic times
    D. whether any data was previously collected from other nearby sites

29. What is the author's opinion of the Euro-centric method mentioned in paragraph 5?
    A. It was unfortunate, but necessary.
    B. It was completely unavoidable.
    C. It was regrettable because it created cultural misunderstandings.
    D. It only took place within a small geographical area.

30. According to the passage, archeological methods:
    A. have developed a good deal when compared to earlier centuries.
    B. need to remain static to be useful.
    C. have been rectified in countries in the Far East.
    D. vary according to local conditions.

A) Visit Abbyville Gardening Center

Wake up your senses with a trip to Abbyville Gardening Center this month.

You can view our herbs and medicinal plants in the herb garden this month for free without an appointment. Come and enjoy the beautiful herbal scent that is carried to the surrounding woodland.

Perhaps you prefer flowers to herbs? Our award-winning florists offer flower arranging courses that you can fit around your busy life. You can learn how to create beautiful arrangements. Call (542) 120 0001 for information and prices.

B) The Positive Effect of Flowers

Recent research shows that interaction with flowers and other botanicals has many benefits for our health. In fact, several recent studies link floral products with human well-being.

Flower arranging not only combines lovely aromas with beautiful colors and textures, but also makes a person feel closer to nature. In addition, floral design is a creative and calming activity that challenges the mind, requiring its participants to focus on visual skills that improve cognition, information processing, and memory.

Another study found that the mere presence of flowers has an immediate effect on mood and happiness. Those in the study who had frequent contact with an environment that had flowers reported more positive moods and less anxiety. Notably, flowers appeared to have the most positive impact upon seniors, reducing depression and encouraging interaction with others.

These beautiful plants help employees to have more enthusiasm and energy at work as well, leading to innovative thinking and more original solutions. Studies like these seem to confirm what I have always known instinctively: that having flowers makes us feel better in many ways.

C) Bees and Flowers

Did you know that flowers and bees share a symbiotic relationship? Yes, that's right! Bees benefit from flowers, but flowers could not flourish without bees.

Most people know that flowers provide bees with the food that the insects need in order to survive. Bees consume the pollen in the flower, as well as the nectar, the sweet liquid substance that flowers produce to attract the bees.

Most bees are social insects that live in colonies of between 10,000 and 60,000 inhabitants. After they collect nectar and pollen from flowers, they fly back to these colonies. They use the nectar to create honey, which then can feed the entire colony.

On the other hand, bees also bring benefits to flowering plants, helping the plants to pollinate and therefore reproduce. Plants cannot seek out mates to create offspring in the same way that animals do. Flowers need to have agents, like bees, birds, and even the wind, to move their genetic material from one plant to another.

Flowering plants have the male part of their genes in their pollen, and when bees fly from flower to flower, they carry and deposit this pollen in other plants in the same species. In this way, flowering plants are able to create seeds and reproduce.

Without bees, pollination and reproduction would be impossible for most of our plant species, so the work of bees is essential to the ecosystems they in which they live. **This** means that we can also enjoy various types of fruits, vegetables, and other plant products that would not be available otherwise.

The following questions refer to section A.

31. What can be inferred about plants in the herb garden?
    A. They all can be used as medicine.
    B. They are very fragrant.
    C. These plants also grow in the woodland.
    D. People prefer them over the flowers.

32. What should someone who wants to take a course in flower arranging do?
    A. Call for more information
    B. Visit Abbyville Garden Center
    C. Inquire at the herb garden
    D. Make an appointment with a gardener

The following questions refer to section B.

33. Why is floral design good for the mind?
    A. It has nice aromas, colors, and textures.
    B. People feel relaxed because they are close to nature.
    C. People have to visualize and think about how to organize the flowers.
    D. It makes its participants happy and in a better mood than before.

34. According to the passage, how is flower arranging good for seniors?
    A. It lessens their anxiety.
    B. It helps them to feel calm.
    C. It makes them feel enthusiastic.
    D. It helps them be more socially active with other people.

35. How does the author feel about flowers?
    A. They are most important for business people.
    B. They can have a positive effect on almost anyone.
    C. Flowers are more beautiful than other botanicals.
    D. Flowers are very beneficial to nature.

The following questions refer to section C.

36. What is the main idea of the passage?
    A. Bees and flowers depend on each another.
    B. Pollination and reproduction are necessary for flowers and bees.
    C. The genes of bees and flowers are very different.
    D. Agents like birds and bees depend on flowers.

37. According to the passage, how do bees benefit from flowers?
    A. They can pollinate more extensively.
    B. They create food from flower pollen and nectar.
    C. They can be more social and attract bees to their colonies.
    D. They become an important part of the ecosystem.

38. According to the passage, why do flowers and other plants need bees?
    A. to help bee colonies expand
    B. to seek out new mates
    C. to correct a genetic flaw
    D. to develop seeds and duplicate

39. In the last paragraph of passage C, what does **This** refer to?
    A. plant species
    B. various types of fruits and vegetables
    C. the work of bees
    D. other plant products

The following question refers to two or more sections.

40. What do human beings gain from other plants besides flowers?
    A. medicines and an increased selection of food
    B. less anxiety and better moods
    C. pollen, honey, and seeds
    D. less pollen in the wind

A) Join Cycling4u Tours

Want to focus on riding and let someone take care of everything else? Then a guided cycle tour might be for you!

Ride for a day or join a full-length cross-country tour to immerse yourself completely in the experience. You can set your own pace, and even novices can ride with the more advanced cyclists without getting left behind.

To embark on an adventure with us, register on our webpage at www.cycling4u.biz

B) Bicycle Safety

Bicycling is an excellent way to exercise, see the natural world, and reduce your carbon footprint. However, bicyclists face many hazards, especially when they share the road with vehicles. Injuries can and do happen, even on a designated cycling path.

The number of deaths from bicycle incidents increased thirty percent from 2010 to the present. Of these bicyclist deaths, seventy percent involved motor vehicles. There are now approximately 80 million bicyclists on the road with motorized vehicles, so it is of paramount importance that bicyclists take safety precautions to protect themselves.

Cyclists would be imprudent not to check their equipment before setting out on any bike ride or journey. The seat should be adjusted and locked in place. It is best to have a rear-view mirror, a horn or bell, and reflectors on the rear, front, pedals, and spokes. When riding after dark, a bright headlight is also recommended. The helmet is often worn incorrectly, thereby offering inadequate protection. It should be adjusted until it fits snugly on the head. Position the sizing pads so that the helmet fits properly. Then place the helmet level on your head, covering the forehead and not tipped backward or forward.

C) How the Bicycle Evolved

All of us are familiar with the modern bicycle, but there were many earlier two-wheeled transportation devices. Several different models preceded the one that we are familiar with today.

In the 16th century, Leonardo da Vinci sketched the designs for a basic bicycle. The German Baron Karl von Drais modernized the basic design in the early 19th century. Named the "velocipede," the device consisted of two metal wheels that were held together with a wooden bar in the center. However, the vehicle had no pedals to propel it, so the rider first had to walk or run to gather speed and then raise his or her legs and continue to ride until the momentum ceased.

Nearly eight years later, two French carriage makers had an idea that would change the cycling world forever: the attachment of pedals to the front wheel and the installation of a driving seat on the central support beam. In addition, their bicycle frames were made from iron instead of wood and featured rubber tires for a more comfortable ride.

After a few years of increased bicycle popularity, Englishman John Kemp Starley invented what he called the "safety bicycle" in 1885. Regarded as one of the most significant inventions in cycling history, it featured a chain that connected the pedals to the rear wheel, which made the front wheel steerable. This device started the era known today as the "Golden Age of the Bicycle."

The following questions refer to section A.

41. What is the main purpose of this text?
    A. to encourage people to be adventurous
    B. to show that cycling can be a social activity
    C. to advertise bike rides and tours
    D. to demonstrate how cycling helps fitness

The following questions refer to section B.

42. What situation does the author mention that is particularly dangerous for cyclists?
    A. using designated cycling paths
    B. failing to have a rear-view mirror
    C. being on the road with automotive traffic
    D. forgetting to wear a helmet

43. Why does the author mention deaths from cycling in paragraph 2?
    A. to provide the reader with a shocking fact
    B. to emphasize the importance of bicycle safety
    C. to demonstrate how inconsiderate drivers of vehicles can be
    D. to criticize those who do not ride and drive safely

44. Why does the author mention the adjustment of the helmet?
    A. Too many people wear it covering the forehead.
    B. Many people wear it incorrectly and ineffectively.
    C. The helmet often fits too tightly and is uncomfortable.
    D. People do not realize that the helmet can move backward or forward.

45. How does the author feel about checking cycling equipment?
    A. It is tedious but necessary.
    B. It should help to reduce cycling deaths in the future.
    C. Drivers of vehicles should be aware of cycling equipment precautions.
    D. Failing to do so is irresponsible.

The following questions refer to section C.

46. What is the main purpose of the article?
    A. to reveal arguments between bicycle inventors
    B. to describe how the bicycle became popular
    C. to talk about the history of the bicycle
    D. to explain how the bicycle became safe

47. Why does the author mention Leonardo da Vinci?
    A. His model was considered very modern for its time.
    B. He helped to design the velocipede.
    C. His design was the basis for later inventions.
    D. It was the earliest form of non-motorized transportation.

48. What problem did riders of the velocipede face?
    A. They were impeded by the central bar.
    B. They disliked the wooden wheels.
    C. They hurt their legs using the device.
    D. They could not travel far on the vehicle.

49. According to the passage, why was Starley's invention an improvement upon its earlier devices?
    A. Riders could change direction.
    B. It could go faster.
    C. It was more comfortable.
    D. It could travel farther.

The following question refers to two or more sections.

50. What would the author of section B probably agree with?
    A. Early versions of the bicycle were extremely unsafe.
    B. Advanced cyclists ride more safely than beginners.
    C. Cyclist are foolish to travel on major roads.
    D. Going on a Cycling4u Tour is a great idea.

PART 4 – MET WRITING PRACTICE TESTS AND SAMPLE ESSAYS

Format of the MET Writing Test

The MET writing test has two parts.

In part 1 of the writing test, you will see a group of three small questions on a familiar topic, such as travel or study.

You should write approximately 40 to 50 words in response to each question on part 1 of the test.

In part 2 of the writing test, you will need to write a longer essay on a different topic. The essay questions on this part of the test usually present a problem, so you will have to write about possible solutions.

You should try to write at least 250 words on part 2 of the writing test, but write an essay longer than this if you can.

You need to write your responses by hand, so be sure that your handwriting is readable. You have 45 minutes to complete all of the tasks on the MET writing test, so you will have to watch the time carefully.

How to Use this Section of the Study Guide

In the following sections, you will see two MET writing test questions with sample responses. Study these samples, paying specially attention to the vocabulary, verb tenses, and sentence structures in each one.

After the two sample questions, you will find ten more practice sets of essay questions. You should try to write responses to each one of the questions, allowing 45 to complete all of the parts of the writing test.

You may want to study the grammar section of this book first, and do the related grammar exercises before attempting the writing tests in this part of the study guide.

You may also wish to purchase our other publication entitled *Michigan English Test Listening and Speaking Study Guide: MET Test Idioms, Exercises, and Practice Tests* to gain knowledge of the idioms and conditional sentence structures that are expected on the MET Test.

Essay Scoring – How Your Essays Are Marked

The six following characteristics of your essays will be assessed:

1. **Clear central idea** – This means that your essay should answer the question that has been posed. You will need to express your main idea in a clear way in the introduction of the essay.

   The examiner reading your essay assesses this aspect of your essay by searching for a thesis statement in the first paragraph of your essay.

   A thesis statement is a sentence in the first paragraph that states the main idea of your essay. It is usually placed in the last sentence of the first paragraph.

2. **Well-supported** – Your essays should demonstrate unity and coherence among the examples that you use in your essay.

   You need to be sure that you provide solutions to the problem presented in the essay question. Your score will not be affected by the opinions you express. It is extremely important to elaborate on the ideas in your essay by giving reasons and examples.

   The examiner reading your essays searches for linking words and phrases that signal that examples or reasons are being provided in the essay. These linking words and phrases include the following: "such as," "for example," "for this reason," and "because of."

3. **Logical organization** – Your essay should be divided into paragraphs, which have been set out in an organized manner. Each body paragraph should contain a certain topic.

You should also include a conclusion that sums up the essay.

The examiner reading your essay looks for logical paragraph divisions, as well as for linking words and phrases which indicate that a new paragraph is beginning.

4. **Writing conventions** – Your essay should be grammatically accurate and punctuated correctly. Your spelling should also be correct.

5. **Syntactic complexity** – You should write long and developed sentences that demonstrate a variety of sentence patterns.

   You should avoid repeatedly beginning your sentences in the same way, such as "I think that."

   The examiner reading your essay will look for a variety of sentence patterns.

6. **Appropriate tone and style** – Your essay needs to address the concerns of your target audience.

   You need to be sure that you have used the correct word choice and style in order to achieve this purpose.

   Generally speaking, the tone of your essay should be formal and academic.

How to Avoid Common Essay Errors and Raise Your Score

In the previous section, we talked about the characteristics of a well-written essay. However, you may also wonder which aspects of an essay would be scored poorly by the person who is evaluating your written work.

These errors most commonly cause students to receive a low score on the MET essay:

1. The essay fails to express a clear point of view or provides a viewpoint that cannot be logically supported.

    Tip: You can avoid this error by giving a clear thesis statement in the first paragraph of your essay.

2. The essay is written in a tone and style that is not suitable for the audience.

    Tip: Using the correct tone and style involves avoiding slang expressions in your writing. Examples of slang language are words like "awesome" or "guy."

3. The reasons or examples provided in the essay are flawed because they do not support the student's main point.

    Tip: Be sure that your reasons and examples are closely related to your main idea and to the essay topic. For instance, if you are asked whether art programs should be supported in schools, and then go on to talk about physical education programs because you believe they are similar to art programs, your reasoning would be flawed.

4. The essay is disorganized and therefore difficult to read and score.

    Tip: You can avoid this error by brainstorming your ideas and planning your essay before you begin writing.

5. The essay contains errors in sentence construction or contains only simple or repetitive sentence structures.

   Tip: Try to avoid writing every sentence of your essay in the subject-verb-object sentence pattern. In order to avoid this shortcoming, you can begin sentences with words and phrases like "although" or "because of this."

6. The essay does not demonstrate a complex thought process.

   Tip: Be sure that you give reasons and examples to express and support your position.

7. The essay contains errors in spelling, grammar, and punctuation.

   Tip: If you have weaknesses in these areas, you should pay special attention to the grammar section of this study guide.

How to Organize and Structure Your MET Essay

Most teachers agree that the best MET essays follow a four or five paragraph format. This format will help to ensure that your essay is well-organized.

This format also helps you write longer and more developed essays that will be over 250 words, instead of just managing a 250-word minimum.

The five-paragraph essay is organized as follows:

Paragraph 1 – This paragraph is the introduction to your essay. It should include a thesis statement that clearly indicates your main idea. It should also give the reader an overview of your supporting points.

Paragraph 2 – The second paragraph is where you elaborate on your first supporting point. It is normally recommended that you state your strongest and most persuasive point in this paragraph.

Paragraph 3 – You should elaborate on your main idea in the third paragraph by providing a second supporting point.

Paragraph 4 – You should mention your third supporting point in the fourth paragraph. This can be the supporting point that you feel to be the weakest.

Paragraph 5 – In the fifth and final paragraph of the essay, you should make your conclusion. The conclusion should reiterate your supporting points and sum up your position.

The four-paragraph essay will follow the same structure as above, with paragraphs 2 and 3 elaborating two key supporting points and paragraph 4 stating the conclusion.

If you decide to put four paragraphs in your essay instead of five, each paragraph should be longer and slightly more detailed than that of a five-paragraph essay.

We will illustrate both the four and five paragraph essay formats in our sample essays in the next section of this study guide.

MET WRITING TEST – SAMPLE RESPONSE 1

PART 1

1. What's your favorite academic subject? Why?

Psychology is the academic subject that I enjoy the most. I especially enjoy studying about human behavior and the different motivations for it. I think learning about and trying to understand the reasons that make human beings tick is absolutely fascinating.

2. What aspect about it do you like best?

Behavioral psychology is appealing to me because it offers insights into how people can develop better habits and communicate more effectively with one another. In the business context, efficient habits and better communication are especially important.

3. Tell us about what you plan to study at college.

I plan on studying behavioral psychology at college. I know it will be difficult because this major has a lot of prerequisites, and there is a great deal of competition just to be accepted for the course. Nevertheless, with hard work, I believe that I can be successful in this field.

PART 2

Recent research has indicated that cycling is much better for our health and for our planet than using motorized vehicles. Yet, most people still use their cars to travel, even for short distances. What can be done to encourage people to cycle? Give reasons and examples to support your opinion.

There is a constant question in society nowadays about the environmental and health risks caused by the use of motorized vehicles. It is irrefutable that increasing regulatory measures would bring about benefits to society. This essay will discuss two measures that the government might take to address the issue.

There is no doubt that countries using non-motorized transport as a norm have a better level of health in the general population. In Denmark, where most people cycle to work, it is reported that levels of heart disease and stroke are far lower than they are in other countries. We only need to look at certain remote villages in the Far East to see the effects of motorized vehicles on our planet.

One can see that levels of air pollution and other forms of environmental contamination are far less in these villages than in so-called "developed" countries. Consider the converse case, for instance, in the United States, where a heavy reliance on motor vehicles has resulted in this country being one of the largest emitters of greenhouse gases in the world.

Perhaps the best solution to the issue at hand is to have the government provide certain incentives to those who decide not to use motorized vehicles. For instance, the government could offer rebates or subsidies on bicycle purchases. Another possible course of action would be to introduce certain fees or fines for vehicle usage, but to establish those controls within very clear limits.

To sum up, one thing is clear: whether by positive reinforcement, as in the first example, or by negative reinforcement as in the second, both remedies take into account the pressing concern of the state of the global environment, as well as protecting the needs of the population for personal health and individual freedom.

ANALYSIS OF SAMPLE 1

Study the sample responses below, paying special attention to the important <u>underlined</u> phrases, the vocabulary in **bold**, and the verb usage in *italics*.

Notice that the essay in part 2 follows the five-paragraph format.

It also gives a clear thesis statement:

> This essay will discuss two measures that the government might take to address the issue.

PART 1

1. What's your favorite academic subject? Why?

Psychology is the academic subject <u>that I enjoy</u> the most. <u>I especially enjoy</u> studying about human behavior and the different motivations for it. <u>I think</u> learning about and trying to understand the reasons that make human being tick is absolutely fascinating.

2. What aspect about it do you like best?

Behavioral psychology <u>is appealing to me</u> because <u>it offers insights into</u> how people can develop better habits and communicate more effectively with one another. In the business context, efficient habits and better communication are <u>especially important</u>.

3. Tell us about what you plan to study at college.

<u>I plan on</u> studying behavioral psychology at college. <u>I know it will be</u> difficult because this major has a lot of prerequisites, and there is a great deal of competition just to be accepted onto the course. Nevertheless, with hard work, <u>I believe that I</u> can be successful in this field.

PART 2

There is a constant question in society nowadays about the environmental and health risks caused by the use of motorized vehicles. It is **irrefutable** that increasing regulatory measures *would bring about* benefits to society. This essay will discuss two measures that the government *might take* to address the issue.

There is no doubt that countries using non-motorized transport as a norm have a better level of health in the general population. In Denmark, where most people cycle to work, it is reported that levels of heart disease and stroke are far lower than they are in other countries. We only need to look at certain remote villages in the Far East to see the effects of motorized vehicles on our planet.

One can see that levels of air pollution and other forms of environmental contamination are far less in these villages than in so-called "developed" countries. Consider the converse case, for instance, in the United States, where a heavy reliance on motor vehicles has resulted in this country being one of the largest emitters of greenhouse gases in the world.

Perhaps the best solution to the issue at hand *is to have* the government provide certain incentives to those who decide not to use motorized vehicles. For instance, the government could offer **rebates** or **subsidies** on bicycle purchases. Another possible course of action *would be to* introduce certain fees or fines for vehicle usage, but to establish those controls within very clear limits.

To sum up, one thing is clear: whether by positive reinforcement, as in the first example, or by negative reinforcement as in the second, both remedies take into account the pressing concern of the state of the global environment, as well as protecting the needs of the population for personal health and individual freedom.

MET WRITING TEST – SAMPLE RESPONSE 2

PART 1

1. What's your favorite thing to do with your family?

My family and I have a favorite game called Jenga that we like to play when we have free time. In this game, you build a miniature tower out of pieces of wood. Then each person takes turns removing blocks from the tower, while trying not to knock the structure down.

2. What do you like about it and why?

I adore playing Jenga because it is a game of both luck and skill. Skill is needed because you can learn which blocks are easiest to remove, and luck also plays a part because your success depends on how damaged the structure already is when your turn comes.

3. Tell us about the last time you did this.

I last played Jenga after Christmas dinner with my mom, dad, brother, and sister. I remember it very well because I lost the game spectacularly on that occasion. The tower was leaning badly when it was my turn, and I managed to topple the entire structure over.

PART 2

With the declining cost of air travel, more people than ever are flying abroad on vacation nowadays. However, this type of tourism brings with it increasing issues for the host countries. What can be done to encourage people to lessen the problems associated with tourism? Give reasons and examples to support your opinion.

Cheaper flights are making it more and more affordable and convenient for people around the world to travel to other countries. In the United States alone, there has been a recent proliferation in low-cost and budget flights to "exotic" destinations. However, in many cases, "exotic" may mean one of the less economically well-off countries of the world. Because this increase in air travel should give us reason to reconsider our vacation plans, two trends have emerged in the travel industry to deal with the problems associated with expanding global tourism.

"Ecotourism," which is aimed at protecting threatened natural environments and intended to support conservation efforts within a host country, is one possible solution to the problem. Eco-travelers realize that human beings are part of the environments they visit, and accordingly, they strive to develop financial benefits and promote human rights for the local inhabitants of the countries to which they travel.

Promoting the rights of and responsibilities to local inhabitants is also the goal of "voluntourism." Traveling in this way involves working as a volunteer in a host country, usually under the auspices of a sponsoring charitable organization. This type of tourism brings benefits to both the traveler and local inhabitants since it allows the tourist to have an adventure, while helping the host country with local issues.

The issues caused by tourism mean that one should devote careful awareness to the effects of one's proposed trip on the host country. All in all, it might appear that "voluntourism" and "ecotourism" will become even more popular in the future as travelers take the issues of the host country into account when deciding where to go on vacation.

ANALYSIS OF SAMPLE 2

Study the sample responses below, paying special attention to the important underlined phrases, the vocabulary in **bold**, and the verb usage in *italics*.

Notice that the essay in part 2 follows a four-paragraph format.

It also gives a clear thesis statement:

> Because this increase in air travel should give us reason to reconsider our vacation plans, two trends have emerged in the travel industry to deal with the problems associated with expanding global tourism.

PART 1

1. What's your favorite thing to do with your family?

My family and <u>I have a favorite</u> game called Jenga that <u>we like to</u> play when we have free time. In this game, you build a miniature tower out of pieces of wood. Then each person takes turns removing blocks from the tower, while trying not to knock the structure down.

2. What do you like about it and why?

<u>I adore</u> playing Jenga because it is a game of both luck and skill. Skill is needed because you can learn which blocks are easiest to remove, and luck also <u>plays a part</u> because your success depends on how damaged the structure already is when your turn comes.

3. Tell us about the last time you did this.

<u>I last</u> played Jenga <u>after</u> Christmas dinner with my mom, dad, brother, and sister. <u>I remember it very well because</u> I lost the game spectacularly on that occasion. The tower was leaning badly when it was my turn, and I managed to topple the entire structure over.

PART 2

Cheaper flights are making it more and more **affordable** and **convenient** for people around the world to travel to other countries. In the United States alone, there has been a recent **proliferation** in low-cost and budget flights to "exotic" destinations. However, in many cases, "exotic" may mean one of the less economically well-off countries of the world. Because this increase in air travel should give us reason to reconsider our vacation plans, two <u>trends have emerged</u> in the travel industry <u>to deal with the problems</u> associated with expanding global tourism.

"Ecotourism," <u>which is aimed at</u> protecting threatened natural environments and intended to support conservation efforts within a host country, **is one possible solution to the problem.** Eco-travelers realize that human beings are part of the environments they visit, and accordingly, they strive to develop financial benefits and promote human rights for the local inhabitants of the countries to which they travel.

Promoting the rights of and responsibilities to local inhabitants is also <u>the goal of</u> "voluntourism." Traveling in this way involves working as a volunteer in a host country, usually under the **auspices** of a sponsoring charitable organization. This type of tourism <u>brings benefits to</u> both the traveler and local inhabitants since it allows the tourist to have an adventure, while helping the host country with local issues.

<u>The issues caused by</u> tourism mean that one should devote careful awareness to the effects of one's proposed trip on the host country. <u>All in all, it might appear that</u> "voluntourism" and "ecotourism" will become even more popular in the future as travelers take the issues of the host country into account when deciding where to go on vacation.

10 MORE MET WRITING PRACTICE TESTS

SET 1

Part 1

1. Who do you admire the most? How often do you see him or her?
2. What qualities do you like in that person?
3. Tell us about the last time you saw him or her.

Part 2

Medical professionals have repeatedly informed us that we should consume at least five portions of fruits and vegetables each day. Nevertheless, many people eat far less than the recommended amount, potentially damaging their health. What can be done to encourage people to eat better? Give reasons and examples to support your opinion.

SET 2

Part 1

1. What is your favorite food? How often do you eat it?
2. What do you like about it?
3. Tell us about the last time you ate it.

Part 2

Recent research indicates that pollution from greenhouse gases is now at critical levels around the world. What can be done to encourage people to recycle and conserve energy? Give reasons and examples to support your opinion.

SET 3

Part 1

1. What things make you laugh? Do you have fun often?
2. Why do you think they are funny?
3. Tell us about the last time you had a good laugh.

Part 2

Much concern has been expressed in the news media recently about people having too much "screen time." What can be done to encourage people to use their computers and watch TV less? Give reasons and examples to support your opinion.

SET 4

Part 1

1. What's your favorite kind of music? How often do you listen to it?
2. What do you like about it?
3. Tell us about the last time you listened to it.

Part 2

Statistics reveal that every year, some students are finishing high school without the mathematical and English language skills necessary for the workplace. What can be done to solve this problem? Give reasons and examples to support your opinion.

SET 5

Part 1

1. What is the best present you ever received? Can you describe it?
2. Who gave it to you and when?
3. Why was it so special?

Part 2

A new study has demonstrated that overeating, particularly eating too much sugar, can cause a number of health problems. What can be done to encourage people to cut down on their calorie consumption? Give reasons and examples to support your opinion.

SET 6

Part 1

1. When are you the happiest? Why?
2. What do you like in particular about these happy occasions or things?
3. Tell us about the last time you were very happy.

Part 2

In spite of knowing that drinking alcohol and smoking can result in cancer and other serious illnesses, many people still choose to drink and smoke. What can be done to encourage people to give up drinking and smoking? Give reasons and examples to support your opinion.

SET 7

Part 1

1. Do you watch movies often? What's your favorite movie?
2. What do you like about it in particular?
3. Tell us about the last movie you saw.

Part 2

According to social scientists, many people interact on their cell phones at the expense of interacting with human beings. What can be done to encourage people to use their phones less and become more social? Give reasons and examples to support your opinion.

SET 8

Part 1

1. Which chore do you dislike doing the most? How often do you have to do it?
2. What do you dislike about it?
3. Tell us about the last time you had to do it.

Part 2

The census has revealed that most families regularly overspend. In fact, some families are now seriously in debt. What can be done to encourage people to spend less? Give reasons and examples to support your opinion.

SET 9

Part 1

1. Which public holiday in your country do you like best? Why?
2. What do you like about it in particular?
3. Tell us about the last time you celebrated it.

Part 2

According to most doctors, stress and worry can cause a number of health issues. However, many of us continue to suffer from anxiety and stress. What can be done to help people feel less stressed and anxious? Give reasons and examples to support your opinion.

SET 10

Part 1

1. How often do you read for leisure? What's your favorite book?
2. What do you like about it?
3. Tell us something about the last book you read.

Part 2

We all know that things often need to be done by a certain time. However, many of us put off even necessary tasks. What can be done to encourage people to stop procrastinating like this? Give reasons and examples to support your opinion.

ANSWER KEYS

Adverbs of Location

1) anyplace / anywhere

2) elsewhere / somewhere else / another place

3) everywhere

4) anyplace else / anywhere else

5) somewhere

6) anyplace / anywhere

7) elsewhere / somewhere else / another place

8) somewhere

9) anywhere else / anyplace else

10) everywhere

Adverbs of Degree

1) enough

2) absolutely

3) far

4) almost / nearly

5) almost / nearly

6) barely

7) almost / nearly

8) hardly

9) even

10) quite

Another / Other / Others

1) another

2) others

3) others

4) others, another

5) other

6) other

7) other

8) others

9) another

10) others

Comparatives and Superlatives

1) the most intelligent

2) more intelligent than

3) more beautiful than

4) the most beautiful of

5) the smartest

6) smarter than

7) harder than

8) the hardest of

9) taller than

10) the tallest

Connectives

Question 1

Answer (1a):

a) In spite of the temperature being quite high yesterday, it really didn't feel that hot outside.

The words "in spite of" are a phrase linker, not a sentence linker, so they take a phrase, not a clause.

The verb "was" needs to be changed to "being" in order to form a present participle phrase.

Answer (1b):

There are two possible answers:

b) The temperature was quite high yesterday. Nevertheless, it really didn't feel that hot outside.

b) The temperature was quite high yesterday; nevertheless, it really didn't feel that hot outside.

"Nevertheless" is a sentence linker. As such, it can be used to begin a new sentence. Alternatively, the semicolon can be used to join the original sentences. If the semicolon is used, the first letter of the word following it must not be capitalized.

Question 2:

Answer (2a):

a) Our star athlete didn't receive a gold medal in the Olympics, although he had trained for competition for several years in advance.

"Although" is a subordinator, so the two sentences can be combined without any changes.

Answer (2b):

b) Despite having trained for competition for several years in advance, our star athlete didn't receive a gold medal in the Olympics.

The two parts of the sentence are inverted, and the verb "had" needs to be changed to "having" to make the present participle form.

Question 3:

Answer (3a):

a) Because of acrimonious relationships within our extended family, our immediate family decided to go away on vacation during the holiday season to avoid these conflicts.

"Because of" is a phrase linker. As such, the subject and verb (there are) need to be removed from the original sentence in order to form a phrase.

Answer (3b):

b) Because there are acrimonious relationships within our extended family, our immediate family decided to go away on vacation during the holiday season to avoid these conflicts.

Answer (3c):

c) Due to the fact that there are acrimonious relationships within our extended family, our immediate family decided to go away on vacation during the holiday season to avoid these conflicts.

"Because" and "due to the fact that" are subordinators, so no changes to the original sentences are required.

The phrase "to avoid these conflicts" can be omitted since this idea is already implied by the words "acrimonious relationships."

Question 4:

Answer (4a):

There are two possible answers.

a) My best friend had been feeling extremely sick for several days. However, she refused to see the doctor.

a) My best friend had been feeling extremely sick for several days; however, she refused to see the doctor.

Answer (4b):

b) My best friend had been feeling extremely sick for several days, but she refused to see the doctor.

"But" is a subordinator, so the two sentences can be combined without any changes.

Question 5:

Answer (5a):

a) While he generally doesn't like drinking alcohol, he will do so on social occasions.

Answer (5b):

"Yet" can be used as both a subordinator and as a sentence linker, so there are three possible answers in this instance.

b) He doesn't like drinking alcohol. Yet, he will do so on social occasions.

b) He doesn't like drinking alcohol; yet, he will do so on social occasions.

b) He doesn't like drinking alcohol, yet he will do so on social occasions.

The difference is that the third sentence places slightly less emphasis on the particular occasions in which he will drink than the other two sentences.

Question 6:

Answer (6a):

"Thus" is a sentence linker, so there are two possible answers:

a) The government's policies failed to stimulate spending and expand economic growth. Thus, the country slipped further into recession.

a) The government's policies failed to stimulate spending and expand economic growth; thus, the country slipped further into recession.

Answer (6b):

b) The government's policies failed to stimulate spending and expand economic growth, so the country slipped further into recession.

"So" is a subordinator. The two sentences may therefore be joined without any changes.

Question 7:

Answer (7a):

There are two possible answers.

a) Even though students may attend certain classes without fulfilling a prerequisite, they are advised of the benefit of taking at least one non-required introductory course.

a) Even though students are advised of the benefit of taking at least one non-required introductory course, they may attend certain classes without fulfilling a prerequisite.

"Even though" is a subordinator, so no changes are needed. It is advisable to change the word "students" to the pronoun "they" on the second part of the new sentence in order to avoid repetition.

The order or the clauses may be changed in the new sentence since there is no cause and effect relationship between the two original sentences.

Answer (7b):

There are two possible answers:

b) Students may attend certain classes without fulfilling a prerequisite. Apart from this, they are advised of the benefit of taking at least one non-required introductory course.

b) Students may attend certain classes without fulfilling a prerequisite; apart from this, they are advised of the benefit of taking at least one non-required introductory course.

"Apart from this" is a sentence linker, so it needs to be used at the beginning of a separate sentence.

Question 8:

Answer (8a):

a) Owing to advances in technology and medical science, infant mortality rates have declined substantially in recent years.

"Owing to" is a phrase linker that shows cause and effect. The cause is advances in technology and medical science, and the effect or result is the decline in infant mortality rates.

Since "owing to" is a phrase linker, the grammatical subject of the original sentence (there) and the verb (have been) are removed when creating the new sentence.

Answer (8b):

b) Since there have been advances in technology and medical science, infant mortality rates have declined substantially in recent years.

"Since" is a subordinator, so you can combine the sentences without making any changes.

Remember to use a comma between the two parts of the sentence.

Question 9:

Answer (9a):

a) It was the most expensive restaurant in town, besides having rude staff and providing the worst service.

"Besides" is a phrase linker, so use the present participle form of both verbs in the second original sentence. Accordingly, "had" becomes "having" and "provide" becomes "providing."

Answer (9b):

There are two possible answers.

b) In addition to being the most expensive restaurant in town, it had rude staff and provided the worst service.

b) In addition to having rude staff and providing the worst service, it was the most expensive restaurant in town.

"In addition to" is a phrase linker, so the present participle forms are used in the phrase containing this word.

The order of the original sentences can be changed since there is no cause and effect relationship between these ideas.

Question 10:

Answer (10a):

a) Instead of punishing the criminal justly and thereby sending out a message to deter potential offenders in the future, the judge decided to grant a lenient sentence.

Answer (10b):

b) Rather than punishing the criminal justly in order to send out a message to deter potential offenders in the future, the judge decided to grant a lenient sentence.

"Instead of" and "rather than" need to be used with the present particle form (punishing).

"Thereby" must be followed by the present participle form (sending).

However, "in order to" needs to take the base form of the verb (send).

Emphatic Form (Do and Did)

1) to go, did swim

2) to treat, does insult

3) don't love, do love

4) don't like, do eat

5) leaving / having left, did arrive

6) loves, does shout

7) repaired, did break down

8) to be, do care

9) to detest, does smoke

10) doesn't have, does sing

Gerunds and Infinitives

1) writing

2) to listen

3) stealing

4) staying up

5) to study

6) to leave

7) to tell

8) going

9) tying

10) to see

11) to play

12) visiting

13) swimming

14) to pack

15) to cry

16) hearing

17) cutting

18) to win

19) having

20) to study

Modal Verbs

1) should

2) could

3) could, may, might

4) should

5) must

6) may, can, could

7) may, might, could

8) must, should

9) must

10) could, might

Negative Adverbial Clauses

1) Not until noon would bread be available at the grocery store. Type 1

2) Only when his truck ran out of gas did Frank realize he had forgotten to fill it up.

   Type 4

3) Never before have I changed a flat tire. Type 3

4) Only when he took off his sunglasses did I realize who he was. Type 4

5) Never in my life have I seen such an exciting football game. Type 3

6) Not a word did John say during the entire drive home. Type 3

7) Rarely does a teenager flunk his driving test the first time. Types 2 and 5

8) Seldom does Jane stay out past midnight. Type 5

9) Only once have I seen the Grand Canyon. Type 1

10) Hardly ever does he have time to see his parents since he has gone away to college. Types 2 and 5

Past Perfect

1) had we gotten; broke down

2) had I finished; rang

3) had told; had

4) tore; had seen

5) saw; had chosen

6) received; had mailed

7) had the fire started; went off

8) had become; left

9) had begun; saw

10) had just said; arrived

Perfect Infinitive

1) to have worn

2) to have passed

3) to have enjoyed

4) to have visited

5) to have been influenced

6) to have known

7) to have won

8) to have been loved

9) to have been

10) to have been changed

The Third Conditional

1) Had Marek driven more carefully, he wouldn't have had an accident.

2) Had Pavel liked the car, she would have bought it.

3) Had I studied for my exam, I would have passed it.

4) Had Dasha worn a sweater, she wouldn't have caught a cold.

5) Had I known you were coming, I would have prepared something to eat.

6) Had Zahra not been so bored by the TV program, she wouldn't have fallen asleep.

7) Had the movie been interesting, I wouldn't have left half-way through.

8) Had I not told my friend he was stupid, he wouldn't have left in a rage.

9) Had he not argued with his boss, he wouldn't have been fired.

10) Had it not rained all night, the football game wouldn't have been canceled.

Pronouns in the Accusative Case

1) me

2) him

3) me

4) she

5) her, me

6) him

7) me

8) her, me

9) me

10) I

Pronouns – Demonstrative and Relative Pronouns

1) which, that

2) who

3) This, which

4) That

5) whose

6) those

7) these

8) whom

9) whose

10) which

Phrasal Verbs – Exercise 1

1) into

2) up

3) up

4) over

5) up

6) down

7) off

8) around

9) away with

10) up with

11) off

12) over

13) down

14) up

15) against

16) away

17) up

18) off

19) over

20) off

21) out

22) off

23) up

24) down on

25) up

26) through

27) up

28) down

29) out

30) up

Phrasal Verbs – Exercise 2

1) C

2) G

3) A

4) J

5) B

6) F

7) D

8) H

9) E

10) I

Phrasal Verbs – Exercise 3

1) H

2) J

3) A

4) E

5) B

6) D

7) C

8) F

9) I

10) G

Phrasal Verbs – Exercise 4

1) A

2) J

3) G

4) E

5) B

6) H

7) C

8) F

9) D

10) I

Prepositions

1) of, to, to

2) from

3) of

4) under

5) of

6) about

7) upon / on

8) by

9) in

10) on

11) with

12) of

13) in

14) for

15) for

16) to

17) with

18) with

19) to

20) by

21) with

22) to

23) for

24) for

25) with

26) with, of

27) of

28) of

29) to, by

30) at

Grammar Review Exercises – Set 1

1) C
2) B
3) A
4) C
5) D
6) A
7) B
8) A
9) C
10) A
11) C
12) B
13) D
14) C
15) B

Grammar Review Exercises – Set 2

1) D
2) D
3) C
4) D
5) C
6) D
7) B
8) C

9) C

10) A

11) B

12) A

13) D

14) C

15) A

Grammar Review Exercises – Set 3

1) A

2) C

3) A

4) B

5) A

6) A

7) C

8) B

9) C

10) A

11) A

12) D

13) B

14) B

15) B

ANSWERS – READING AND GRAMMAR PRACTICE TEST 1

1) The correct answer is A. We need the noncomparative adjective "anywhere" because we are not making a comparison in the sentence.

2) The correct answer is B. We are indicating that the job is nearly done, so we need the adverb of degree "almost."

3) The correct answer is D. The emphatic form is needed here because we are contrasting the accident to the carefulness. The action is in the past, so the correct answer is "did have."

4) The correct answer is B. We need the accusative form "me" because of the preposition "between."

5) The correct answer is C. The plural form is required because of the plural noun "people" earlier in the sentence.

6) The correct answer is A. The relative pronoun "whose" is correct since the name belongs to the student.

7) The correct answer is B. We are describing a strong obligation or expectation in the recent past, so we need to use "should have" in this sentence.

8) The correct answer is A. We know that the superlative form is needed in this sentence because of the article "the."

9) The correct answer is D. The connective "in spite of that" is needed because of the word "but," which shows a contrast is going to be made. The other answer choices are not grammatically correct.

10) The correct answer is D. This is a form of the third conditional, so the inverted form of the past perfect "had I had" is the correct answer.

11) The correct answer is A. The verb "decide" takes the infinitive, so "to attend" is the correct answer. Notice that the verb "attend" in this context is a transitive verb, so we don't need a preposition.

12) The correct answer is C. "Get away with" means to escape the consequences of your actions.

13) The correct answer is B. The verb "be" is needed after the modal verb "can." We are describing an action, so we need the adverb "easily" rather than the adjective "easy."

14) The correct answer is C. "Not a word" is a negative adverbial clause, so we need to invert the auxiliary verb "did" to get the correct answer "did he say."

15) The correct answer is B. The word "all" needs the preposition "of." The definite article is needed because we are describing something specific, i.e., the new merchandise.

16) The correct answer is A. The passive form of the perfect infinitive is required since we have the verb "are believed."

17) The correct answer is B. The noun phrase "the beginning" needs to be preceded by the preposition "at."

18) The correct answer is A. We need the third conditional form in this sentence since we have the past perfect "hadn't eaten." Remember that you can use "might" instead of "would" in the third conditional.

19) The correct answer is B. We need the singular demonstrative pronoun "this" because the noun "book" is singular.

20) The correct answer is C. The need the plural form "others" because of the word "many."

21) The correct answer is D. The first paragraph states: "very few understand the facts behind these weather events. Even fewer people are aware of how to protect themselves and their property if a tornado were to strike."

22) The correct answer is C. The paragraph goes on to explain that tornadoes are classified into groups, so we can assume that there are many tornadoes.

23) The correct answer is A. The topic sentence states: "tornadoes can be classified as weak, strong, or violent."

24) The correct answer is C. The last paragraph says: "To protect themselves, residents should go to the basement their homes." The basement is the underground floor.

25) The correct answer is D. The author emphasizes that tornadoes result in "loss of life" in paragraph 2 and states that "tornadoes have serious consequences for communities and their inhabitants" in paragraph 3.

26) The correct answer is A. Paragraph 2 states that the figures were of national importance, instead of merely popular. "Frivolous" and "unimportant" are synonyms.

27) The correct answer is A. The second sentence of paragraph 2 states that Robinson "proposed that the work be dedicated to popular figures who were prominent in the western United States." If these people were prominent and popular, we can assume that they were well-known and loved.

28) The correct answer is B. The topic sentence of paragraph 3 states: "Mount Rushmore therefore became a national memorial dedicated to the four presidents who were considered most pivotal in United States' history." "Pivotal" means very important or significant.

29) The correct answer is A. Paragraph 4 states that Borglum decided that is was "best to work on only one head at a time, in order to make each one compatible with its surroundings. To help him visualize the final outcome, he fashioned a 1.5-meter-high plaster model on a scale of 1 to 12." The author makes these comments to emphasize the artist's talent and perception.

30) The correct answer is D. The last paragraph says that "the financing for the project was provided mainly from national government funds." "Federal" from answer choice D means national.

31) The correct answer is C. We know that the Seatown Aquarium has been closed for a certain time period recently because the event is described as the "Grand Reopening."

32) The correct answer is D. Anyone who wants to visit with their children for half-price should bring the coupon with them when they visit the aquarium. Text A states: "any children you accompany can enter for half-price when you present this coupon."

33) The correct answer is B. The characteristic that all fish have in common is a backbone. Text B states that "they have a spine. So, all fish are vertebrates." Spine and vertebrae are synonyms for backbone.

34) The correct answer is A. The author mentions that the seahorse has a very unusual appearance. Text B states: "Other species, like the seahorse, are so bizarre they almost seem other-worldly."

35) The correct answer is B. Fish have evolved by having some heightened senses. Text B states: "Fish are unique on the evolutionary scale" because they "rely . . . more on their hearing, taste, and smell."

36) The correct answer is D. The main idea of the passage is that the athletic performance of some animals is superior to that of humans. Text C states: "the

athletic training and performance of human beings seem unimpressive, paling in comparison to the phenomenal feats performed naturally by members of the animal kingdom."

37) The correct answer is A. People sometimes need special diving equipment because the human body is not designed to cope underwater like fish can. Text C states: "However, the human body can withstand underwater depths up to only 2,300 feet." "Withstand" means able to cope.

38) The correct answer is D. The author mentions penguins to point out a surprising fact. Text C emphasizes that the penguin is "not even a member of the fish species." The words "not even" are used to express surprise.

39) The correct answer is B. The author feels that the athletic performance of animals is remarkable and extraordinary. The author uses words like "phenomenal" to describe animal performance, but uses the words "unimpressive" and "paltry" to describe the performance of humans.

40) The correct answer is C. The author of section B would most strongly agree with the statement that animal performance has developed because of evolution. That is because the author of text B describes the characteristics of the evolution of fish.

41) The correct answer is D. The main purpose of the text is to describe an offer. The offer is that customers can get a coffee for free.

42) The correct answer is B. The author mentions that high cholesterol can be caused by drinking coffee. Text B says that "we have known for a few years now that coffee can elevate blood pressure and also lead to high cholesterol."

43) The correct answer is C. Coffee can cause stomach ache because it makes acidity levels in the stomach higher. Text B explains that "coffee stimulates the secretion of gastric acid, which can lead to stomach upset."

44) The correct answer is A. The author mentions anxiety and depression to exemplify another problem caused by drinking too much coffee. We know this because it describes "health problems like anxiety and depression."

45) The correct answer is A. **This** refers to the fact that sweet things taste less sweet. Text B states that "coffee changes our sense of taste, making sweet things seem less sweet. This may cause us to crave more sweets."

46) The correct answer is B. The main purpose of the article is to discuss fair trade coffee pricing, classification, and consumer outcomes. The first two paragraphs talk about the monetary aspects, paragraph 3 and 4 describe the classification, and paragraph 5 talks about the effect on the consumer.

47) The correct answer is A. The author mentions certification fees and prices to explain the costs and problems for farmers. The problem for farmers is that they have to figure out how best to sell their coffee.

48) The correct answer is B. Fair trade is related to coffee quality in that it has had a negative effect on the quality. Text C states: "Coffee beans sold as fair trade can come from any quality category of coffee, so farmers use lower quality coffee as fair trade."

49) The correct answer is D. The author feels that fair trade coffee has had some unfortunate and unexpected outcomes. Text C states that it causes an "unsatisfactory experience for the consumer and undermines the effort of the farmer and fair trade organizations."

50) The correct answer is C. Coffee production and consumption can cause issues for consumers and farmers. Text B describes the health issues for consumers, and text C describes quality issues for consumers and farmers.

ANSWERS – READING AND GRAMMAR PRACTICE TEST 2

1) The correct answer is C. We have the negative adverbial "very rarely" so we need to invert the auxiliary verb for the correct form "does she appear."

2) The correct answer is A. The relative pronoun "that" is correct since there is a clause after the gap.

3) The correct answer is C. "Size up" is a phrasal verb that means to measure or estimate something.

4) The correct answer is A. The verb "hope" takes the infinitive form, so the correct answer is "to go." The perfect infinitive in answer choice D is incorrect because we are speaking about an action in the future.

5) The correct answer is C. "No sooner" is a negative adverbial, so we need to invert the auxiliary verb for the correct form "had we arrived."

6) The correct answer is D. The verb "recover" takes the preposition "from."

7) The correct answer is B. We have the third conditional here because of the verb "wouldn't have gotten." So, the past perfect "had she been" is needed in the second part of the sentence. We have not used the word "if," so we need to put the auxiliary verb "had" before the pronoun "she."

8) The correct answer is B. We can omit the use of a relative pronoun in this sentence. The correct word order is subject + verb + adverb, so we need the answer "I saw last week."

9) The correct answer is D. We need the bare form of the passive infinitive "be invited" because of the use of the verb "requested" and the relative pronoun "that."

10) The correct answer is C. The superlative form (without "the") is needed here because of the phrase "one of" earlier in the sentence.

11) The correct answer is A. We are talking about a strong obligation in the recent past, so the correct answer is "you should have filled."

12) The correct answer is B. We are making a comparison in this sentence to McDonald's, so we need the comparative adverb of place "somewhere else."

13) The correct answer is D. We need "most" because we are describing the majority of students.

14) The correct answer is A. The verb "deny" takes the gerund form, so "stealing" is the correct answer.

15) The correct answer is C. "Put up with" is a phrasal verb that means to tolerate something or someone.

16) The correct answer is B. We need the phrase linker "because of" since the gap is followed by a phrase, rather than a clause.

17) The correct answer is A. The word "other" is used to modify the plural noun "hobbies."

18) The correct answer is B. The emphatic form "do need" is correct since we are emphasizing a generalization or habit.

19) The correct answer is B. The active form of the perfect infinitive form "to have worked" is correct since the sentence is talking about an action in the recent past.

20) The correct answer is A. The pronouns "you and he" are needed he since they form the subject of this clause in the sentence.

21) The correct answer is B. The author's main purpose is to emphasize the significance of Newton's and Einstein's achievements. Paragraph 2 states: "It is because of Newton's work that we currently understand the effect of gravity on the earth as a global system." The author concludes the passage as follows: "Numerous subsequent investigations into and tests of the theory of general relativity have unequivocally supported Einstein's groundbreaking work."

22) The correct answer is C. "Flash of inspiration" means that a single event caused a positive outcome. It is the opposite of the phrase "slowly developed over time."

23) The correct answer is A. The paragraph states that there is "declining mass and density of the planet from the equator to the poles." "Mass" is similar to weight, so if the weight gets less as we go to the poles, the weight is more near the equator.

24) The correct answer is B. Paragraph 3 states: "Newton remained perplexed about the causes of the power implicit in the variables of his mathematical equations on gravity. In other words, he was unable adequately to explain the natural forces upon which the power of gravity relied. "Reservation" from answer choice B means confusion or doubt. It is close in meaning to the word "perplexed" and the phrase "unable adequately to explain" from the passage. In other words, Newton had a research question that he could not answer.

25) The correct answer is D. Paragraph 4 states that Einstein's work was "revolutionary" and "groundbreaking." Both of these statements describe ideas that were somewhat ahead of their time.

26) The correct answer is A. This is a main idea question. The main body paragraphs describe how a site is treated and how findings are interpreted. It uses the adjectives "uniformly" and "arduous" to describe the process. It also describes this as a "meticulous and lengthy process" in the second sentence of paragraph 3.

27) The correct answer is B. The meaning of this word is revealed in the next sentence in paragraph 4: "the mechanism goes back and forth in this way."

28) The correct answer is D. Paragraph 2 states: "A logical locality to begin searching is one near a site in which artifacts have been found previously."

29) The correct answer is C. The author's opinion about the Euro-centric method is that it was regrettable because it created cultural misunderstandings. Paragraph 5 states: "Lamentably, the misapprehension that the *homo sapiens* species was European in origin began to take shape both in the archeological and wider communities at that time." The word "lamentably" shows regret. The word "misapprehension" indicates a misunderstanding.

30) The correct answer is A. The first sentence of the passage states: "The discipline of archeology has been developing since wealthy Europeans began to plunder relics from distant lands in the early nineteenth century."

31) The correct answer is B. We can infer that the plants in the herb garden are very fragrant. Text A states that there is a "beautiful herbal scent that is carried to the surrounding woodland."

32) The correct answer is A. Someone who wants to take a course in flower arranging should call for more information. Text A advises to "call (542) 120 0001 for information and prices."

33) The correct answer is C. Floral design is good for the mind because people have to visualize and think about how to organize the flowers. Text B explains that floral design requires "its participants to focus on visual skills." Notice that the question is asking about floral design in particular, rather than flowers in general.

34) The correct answer is D. Flower arranging is good for seniors because it helps them be more socially active with other people. Text B says that flowers "have the most positive impact upon seniors, reducing depression and encouraging interaction with others."

35) The correct answer is B. The author feels that flowers can have a positive effect on almost anyone. Text B concludes as follows: "studies like these seem to confirm what I have always known instinctively: that having flowers makes us feel better in many ways."

36) The correct answer is A. The main idea of the passage is that bees and flowers depend on each another. Text C begins as follows:" Did you know that flowers and bees share a symbiotic relationship? Yes, that's right! Bees benefit from flowers, but flowers could not flourish without bees."

37) The correct answer is B. Bees benefit from flowers because they create food from flower pollen and nectar. This is mentioned in paragraphs 2 and 3.

38) The correct answer is D. Flowers and other plants need bees in order to develop seeds and duplicate. This is explained in paragraphs 4 and 5.

39) The correct answer is C. In text C, "This" refers to the work of bees. The previous phrase in the passage states that "the work of bees is essential."

40) The correct answer is A. From other plants besides flowers, human beings gain medicines and an increased selection of food. Text A mentions medicinal plants, and text C talks about fruits, vegetables, and other plant products.

41) The correct answer is C. The main purpose of text A is to advertise bike rides and tours. Text A states: "Ride for a day or join a full-length cross-country tour to immerse yourself completely in the experience."

42) The correct answer is C. The author mentions that being on the road with automotive traffic is particularly dangerous for cyclists. Paragraph 2 states that seventy percent of fatal cycling accidents involved motor vehicles.

43) The correct answer is B. The author mentions deaths from cycling in paragraph 2 to emphasize the importance of bicycle safety. After mentioning the deaths, the author states "so it is of paramount importance that bicyclists take safety precautions to protect themselves."

44) The correct answer is B. The author mentions the adjustment of the helmet because many people wear it incorrectly and ineffectively. In paragraph 3 of text B, the author says: "The helmet is often worn incorrectly, thereby offering inadequate protection."

45) The correct answer is D. The author feels that failing to check cycling equipment is irresponsible. The first sentence of paragraph 3 says: "Cyclists would be imprudent not to check their equipment before setting out on any bike ride or journey." Imprudent and irresponsible are synonyms.

46) The correct answer is C. The main purpose of text C is to talk about the history of the bicycle. We know this because the text is written in chronological order, beginning in the 16th century and ending in the modern day.

47) The correct answer is C. The author mentions Leonardo da Vinci because his design was the basis for later inventions. Text C states: "In the 16th century, Leonardo da Vinci sketched the designs for a basic bicycle. The German Baron Karl von Drais modernized the basic design in the early 19th century."

48) The correct answer is D. Riders of the velocipede faced the problem that they could not travel far on the vehicle. Text C explains that "the rider first had to walk or run to gather speed and then raise his or her legs and continue to ride until the momentum ceased." Momentum means forward movement.

49) The correct answer is A. Starley's invention an improvement upon its earlier devices because riders could change direction. The last paragraph of text C says that "it featured a chain that connected the pedals to the rear wheel, which made the front wheel steerable."

50) The correct answer is A. The author of section B would probably agree with the idea that early versions of the bicycle were extremely unsafe. In text C, we learn that the first bicycles did not have pedals and could not be steered and that the "safety bicycle" wasn't invented until 1885.

Printed in Great Britain
by Amazon